Presence in Relationship

Presence
in
Relationship

Offering Core Process
Psychotherapy

Susan Groves

Reach
PUBLISHERS

Published by Author using Reach Publishers' services,
P O Box 1384, Wandsbeck, South Africa, 3631

Edited by Gil Harper for Reach Publishers
Cover designed by Reach Publishers
Website: www.reachpublishers.co.za
E-mail: reach@webstorm.co.za

Contact the author at
www.susangroves.com

Reach
PUBLISHERS

In appreciation

Sean and the Karuna Institute

Foreword

Core Process is a long-established and highly re-garded form of psychotherapy, one that draws on Buddhist teachings and western psychology, weaving them together into a practical and effec-tive way of working. Core Process was an early pioneer of mindfulness practice, long before it became a widely accepted, mainstream psycho-logical tool. Susan Groves is an experienced Core Process practitioner and her writing offers an unusually accessible insight into depth psycho-therapy. Her conversational, open style invites a personal connection with the reader that helps to reveal the profundity of what can take place be-tween psychotherapist and client when nothing very much seems to be happening. She captures the extraordinary, which can reveal itself from within the apparently mundane at any time, in a direct and vivid manner. Her verbatim pieces of client/therapist process are well chosen, and the inherent possibility of insight into early wounding and the transformation of deep suffering that is held in every moment, is tangible.

Sean Maloney, senior practitioner in Core Process Psychotherapy and former trainer at the Karuna Institute

Table of Contents

Preface

It has been my huge privilege to have been significantly entangled with Christianity and Buddhism over the course of my life. And, in the last decade and a half, to have trained in and practiced Core Process Psychotherapy. I feel Core Process is unique in working with great simplicity and yet profound depth with oneself and others. I will be supported by these three traditions in my writing. I attempt here to write what I know about Core Process Psychotherapy. Perhaps because of the subtle nature of the work which can be experienced as non-linear and non-cognitive, relatively little has been written about it. I'll be drawing on my own experience, including citing examples from my client practice.

Susan Groves
Cape Town
15 December 2014

PART
1

Malaise in relationship

> The malaise in relationship in the West, and the ubiquitous nature of personal and societal trauma, calls for urgent action.

These are the words of Maura Sills, the founder of the Karuna Institute, in the introduction to the handbook for the MA in Core Process Psychotherapy 2002-3, the year of my enrolment in the training.[1]

She goes on to say that:

> Core Process Psychotherapy offers a way in which the healing of this dissonance, fragmentation and disconnection can occur.[2]

That there is a malaise in relationship in the West is something I know for sure.[3] It's something I have known in myself. And that Core Process Psychotherapy has something to offer this condition I know too, having been trained in this modality and now offering this practice to others.

People who have completed the short training programme I offer, have affirmed that this practice is too valuable to be kept in the therapist's room. It has implications for the wounds between us as people and how we relate to our planetary home.

Reflection:

Do you agree/disagree with the statement that there is a malaise – an unease – in relationship in the West? If you disagree, how might you put it differently?

An ennobling truth

Let me jump right in and say something about what may be regarded as one of the central teachings of Buddhism. (I am necessarily communicating my own understanding of the teachings. There will be many Buddhists and scholars who will differ with the way I am putting it.) Buddhism is the root from which Core Process Psychotherapy grew and developed.

You will typically hear that Buddhism is based on the four noble truths. And these are usually described as follows:

1. There is *dukkha* – loosely translated as unsatisfactoriness or suffering.

2. This suffering can be known.[4]

3. Suffering can cease.[5]

4. There is a path that leads to this cessation.[6]

The teaching on the four ennobling truths is said to have come from the first discourse of Siddhartha Gautama – who became known as the Buddha – given in response to his friends' request that he explain to them the understandings he had arrived at.

In Core Process Psychotherapy we explore particularly the first two of these truths – that there is suffering and that it can be known.

I well remember the relief many of us felt on reading Morton Scott Peck's first work, *The Road Less Travelled*, which begins: 'Life is difficult'. Somehow there's such relief in these words. As if, oh, so it's not that things are wrong and wrong with *me*. It is just this: life is difficult. There is *dukkha*.

The Buddha speaks of three characteristics of existence – that it is impermanent, imperfect and impersonal.[7] The imperfect – *dukkha* – we have spoken about: we aren't experiencing what we'd like to be experiencing. The impersonal *(annata)* points out that our particular experience is not (in some sense) unique but rather part of the human condition. To remember this can be helpful. The impermanent *(anicca)* is just that: whatever state one is experiencing, it will change. This doesn't always comfort one in the midst of what may feel like quite intractable spaces, but even just telling oneself this may help a little. A day or two later we will (usually) know that this is true as our mind/

Presence in Relationship

heart/body state will have altered.[8]

This teaching can sound strange and quite obscure but it does allow for a certain spaciousness and openness in enquiry – individually and in relationship – which you may be able to sense more as you read on.

Reflection:

What do you make of the statement that there is *dukkha*/unsatisfactoriness? Is there any comfort in actually stating this?

Do you have any resonance with the three characteristics mentioned here – that of impermanence, the impersonal and imperfect?

Buddhism as the foundation of Core Process Psychotherapy or 'it all belongs together'

Core Process Psychotherapy is often described as a synthesis of western psychology and Buddhist understanding. There are many different traditions within Buddhism, and Core Process draws from a variety of these.

The founders of the Karuna Institute, the home of Core Process Psychotherapy, are Maura and Franklyn Sills. The Institute is highly respected and is one of the first places in the world to offer a mindfulness-based psychotherapy training. In England it falls under the UK Council for Psychotherapy and plays an active role in its affairs. While Franklyn is also involved in other modalities – in particular craniosacral therapy – it is Maura who has been mainly responsible for developing the teachings. I will necessarily be referring to them both regularly in this work.

Maura sees Core Process as an (ongoing) experiment to see whether a 'one person' awareness practice can become a 'two person' practice.

> To discover what arises when the process of meditative inquiry is pursued in relationship – the move from one cushion ... to two ... people looking at each other.[9]

Two people following awareness together.

She regards Core Process as practicing awakening in relationship. She refers to it as a radical teaching[10] and as being quite different from mainstream psychotherapy.[11] I certainly experience Core Process as a fresh and radical paradigm. I feel the world is in need of it. It is the only model I know well in terms of working at depth with the individual. But when I sit with people who have been trained in other modalities, its difference from these becomes very clear to me. Maura regards Core Process as based on the teaching, practice and ethics of Buddhism.[12] She and Franklyn feel that knowing the lineage of something is important.[13] I would agree with this. I always acknowledge that Core Process arises from the lineage of Buddhism. However, many of the mystical or contemplative traditions – found perhaps within all the faiths – do not, I feel, occupy territory very different from Buddhism.

While Core Process is said to be a synthesis, as I have mentioned, of western psychology and Buddhism, I found, in the training, the emphasis far more on contemplation than on western psychology. In some of her writing, Maura acknowledges this emphasis.

She spoke passionately in an interview about how she sees the relationship between Buddhism and psychotherapy:

> Current western psychotherapy is different from Buddhism, in as much as ninety percent of it does not acknowledge anything other than personality... I feel less and less that we have to dip into western psychology for understandings that we can't find within Buddhism itself.[14]

And further:

> Whatever psychotherapy develops in the West, if it truly includes the

centrality of the spiritual journey, it must be encouraged and supported by all of us. My fear is that the existing milieu of psychotherapy in the West, because it's becoming so good at working with personality, is not on the right track... I'm not trying to knock psychotherapy, but if we're not going to include non-duality as a basic foundation of our practice we are headed in the wrong direction, towards a split, heading away from interconnectedness and real responsibility.[15]

One of the trainees on a recent training programme I offered, was Denise. I so well remember – and appreciate – her remark when we met for an interview prior to the training. She had been at a talk I gave about three years previously at the non-governmental agency where she works. I was introducing Core Process Psychotherapy to a group of about 30 people. Referring back to this presentation, she said: 'I was just so excited realising that it all belonged together.'

What Denise was saying was that yes, her spirituality, her interest in the wellbeing of the person, the territory we've called psychology – this and more – it all belongs together. We don't have to do contortion tricks anymore and act as if a part of us doesn't exist. It all belongs together! I hope this book will give you a sense of this.

Reflection:

Do you have a sense of what Denise means when she says 'it all belongs together'? What is your experience of this?

Do you have the experience of a model or paradigm that can hold this 'all-togetherness' for you? If not, is it something you long for?

The particular contribution of Core Process Psychotherapy

The contribution of Core Process Psychotherapy to the field of spirituality and psychology will, I trust, become evident as you go through this book. I will make some remarks here of an introductory nature.

Core Process Psychotherapy is defined as an exploration of how we are in our present experience, and how this expresses the past conditioning and conditions of our lives.

In *Licking Honey from the Razor's Edge,* Maura speaks of Core Process as being based on a completely different set of premises to mainstream psychotherapy.[16] I would entirely agree with this. This does not mean that Core Process is not in conversation with other forms of psychotherapy – of which there are many – and cannot be informed and enriched by these. If one were to observe a Core Process Psychotherapy session, it may not look very different from another more mainstream session. But, in fact, what is happening within it is very different – certainly for the therapist.[17]

There is something about the cognitive approach that is important to mention as we start out. Maura speaks with clarity on the nuanced matter of how we can so easily live in concepts without having a lived understanding of these. In the essay I refer to above, she says the following:

> One of the greatest difficulties in working with Westerners is that they believe that because they have a concept of something they know it. A concept is not the truth, it is not experience. A concept can be helpful. It can point us to some enquiry. If I have a concept of spaciousness that is very helpful... But if I don't have an experience of spaciousness, of openness, then it is not alive, it is not real... Westerners tend to believe that cognitive understanding and conceptual awareness constitute reality.[18]

I so appreciate Maura's ability to articulate these subtle spaces. She has beautifully said of Core Process – and I use this wording often on my flyers – that:

The practitioner often finds themselves at the edge of what can be understood and named by the cognitive mind. We... develop trust in a deeper more nameless intelligence.[19]

She remarks elsewhere that:

Perhaps the most powerful impact of psychotherapy is in the contact that is happening non-verbally, despite whatever we *want* to do.[20]

Many people practising different forms of psychotherapy would agree with this statement but they may then proceed to layer a lot of theoretical material on top of it so that, in fact, its importance is often lost.

Reflection:

What is your response to what you have read here? It can be difficult to 'get a handle' on. If so, don't worry.

Notice if there's any part of you that feels some sort of yearning or 'yes' even if you don't feel you yet understand what you're reading.

Allow yourself to be touched by the material. It's non-cognitive, remember!

Presence in Relationship

Resourcing

I come now to material I deal with early in the training I offer – as it was similarly dealt with at the start of the training I received. It forms an important and ongoing basis for the work of the practitioner and is central to the work with the client.

In the first of the six-session training programme I offer (over a period of four months), I ask the group the following questions: what settles you? What helps you know you're okay? Individually we explore, with paper and crayons, what might emerge on this particular day in response to these questions. I find that the questions themselves begin to settle me.

But it wasn't always this way. When this aspect was introduced into the first part of our training – where do you find resource? – I underestimated its value. Now many years on, it feels important to return to this repeatedly.

Resourcing can be regarded as the answer to the question: what helps? And yes, it includes the acknowledgment that help is necessary.

The difficulty can be that it may feel shameful to need help at all. Some of us grew up not getting the support we needed when we needed it. So we 'grew up' more than we should have, and 'need' wasn't something we could easily welcome. It can be a long journey for many of us before we are able to orient to what helps.[21] And this is indeed part of the ongoing enquiry with the client: *what helps*?

The answers to this may be of an infinite variety. In *Buddha's Brain* by Hanson and Mendius there is a section entitled *Finding refuge*.[22] You might ask yourself: where have I found refuge? Do you remember a time or times of feeling settled, at rest? What were the circumstances or the variables then that allowed for that sense of ease and safety? You may remember sitting quietly in a church. Or lying under a particular tree on your own or with someone with whom you were comfortable. Having the bathroom to yourself as you bath may come to mind for a busy parent. For another it's having a quiet cup of tea. One can also look more broadly here to include aspects of lifestyle: what helps me live in a way that I'm not too unsettled? I think this is an important question to ask at this time on our rather frenetic planet.

One may feel that the simplicity of this exercise is a bit outrageous. In this regard, I like to tell the story from the Bible about a king with a skin disease who approached Elijah, the renowned prophet. Elijah instructs the king to bathe in the Jordan River to receive his healing. The king objects, asking, 'Surely there are better rivers?' Typically what helps is simple. And so can easily escape us.

The word 're-sourcing' can be broken down into returning again to source – so returning to our inherent goodness and health – or to our source, our God, if that is helpful language for us. Re-creation is another word I like – what helps one re-create oneself? What might comfort me?

Asking these questions may be difficult in themselves. For many of us, accessing safety, intimacy, comfort and the nurture we need, is novel and, as I have suggested, may be regarded as shameful. Being open to enquiring into what can help, what can give one comfort, is a hugely useful life skill. I will be speaking of it more later in the book as a key help in dealing with difficulty and trauma in life.

Sometimes one can't find help on one's own. At times comfort can only come in the presence of another. Maura speaks of how, if after a session with a client she is left feeling lousy and inadequate, she is helped by her (then) teenage daughter saying: 'It's alright mom, you're not a bad person.'[23]

Let me share an example from client work.

Teresa is 42 years old. When she was 11, her mother's husband (the client's stepdad) sexually assaulted her repeatedly. At this time, she developed a form of rheumatoid arthritis in her young body.

Now many years on, Teresa is happily married and feels ready to explore the abuse she suffered and the impact it has had and continues to have on her life. She is part of a well-designed group programme for women survivors of childhood sexual abuse.[24] As part of this, she is in one-to-one counselling for the duration of the 12-week programme. She meets with me every week. Her bones ache as her body remembers her experience as a young girl.

'I remember twisting pastry to make jam tarts

with my gran,' she tells me.[25]

Such an evocative image – of jam and pastry and companionable work. This memory is a resource for Teresa. It is helpful for me too to know this so that I don't lose sight of the goodness that has been – and is – in Teresa's life, even as we traverse material that has almost no words, few images, but lots of terror.

I have acknowledged that there may be a sense of artificiality to this practice of resting in resource. This is true. It's a new practice for most of us. There's something about what is called our triune brain that is geared for trouble! We share a large part of the makeup of our brain with the animal world and it makes us on the alert for danger. So a practice that helps us know – right in our cells – that we are safe is one that can take a lot of cultivating.

There may be places we can access in our bodies that help us know we're okay – such as a breath that seems to come from our bellies. This always feels like first prize, as this you can take around with you – if you remember! For some people, it may be bringing the thought of a loved one to mind. Maura, addressing the conference

Mindfulness & Beyond, spoke of steadying herself in the resources of gratitude and good friendship to help settle herself as she prepared to give her address. More broadly, as I have suggested, it may be the lifestyle one chooses – and protects – that is resourcing.

Many of the examples I have given of resourcing include the body. This is surely no coincidence. Might this then be what resourcing essentially is? A return to the body? A key aspect seems to be the body at rest.[26] So in the example I've given of the woman remembering herself as a girl twisting pastry for jam tarts with her granny, I imagine her body was at ease. There was a sense of safety in the presence of her grandmother. She was not on alert for danger. Difficulties and emotional injury have an impact on the body, as we'll explore later in this text. Resourcing provides a way of holding, of healing. Perhaps each time we 'return' we are building our healing, sort of cell by cell. Resourcing is finding the memories or activities that allow the body to fully relax. Whether the resourcing is an action one does or something one calls to mind, the result would be the same. A body at rest. A sense of safety. What helps us to return there? In returning to body we return to earth or the earth element, our wider resource.

The theme of resourcing will be woven through-out this book.

Reflection:

What do you think about the encouragement to find that which settles you? Is it too simplistic? Is it something you could consider taking seriously, even for a day?

If you think back over the last month, can you think of anything that helped you settle? Sitting by a dam, for example. Or humming quietly to your-self? Phoning a friend? Or just sitting and noticing that your breathing is deep and you feel alright?

Would there be any point in building these 'set-tling spaces' into your day, your week, your month? If so, how might you do this? Who might help to remind you?

The *brahmaviharas*

The wonderful thing about Core Process Psychotherapy is that, as a practitioner, one does not do the work on one's own. One rests in the *brahmaviharas*.

The *what?*

Siddhartha Gautama lived about 2,500 years ago in what was called the Vedic culture. The *brahmaviharas* were part of that culture and the Buddha included these in his teaching. Mind you, many Buddhists you speak to would never have heard of them. Buddhism – like many traditions – has diverse schools and the teachings vary considerably.[27]

The word *brahmavihara* means divine abidings. My translation is: good qualities to hang out with. The four qualities are: *metta* which translates as loving kindness; *karuna* meaning compassion; *uppekha* or equanimity; and *mudita* which is sympathetic joy. Formerly, the Core Process training used to advise holding three qualities – clarity, spaciousness and compassion. While these are beautiful, there's something about the four-fold nature of the *brahmaviharas* that is helpful.

These four qualities are part of who we are as human beings. They are also part of our wider reality. One is not trying to rev up qualities that are unnatural to us, but rather calling to mind that which is our essential nature. We rest in qualities that are part of us and are also outside us. This is where Core Process begins and ends really. Without the *brahmaviharas* there is no business!

Of course, this is just one model but I have found it a useful one though it was new to me when I began the training, and my background is more in the Christian tradition. One can attribute these qualities to God if that feels helpful.

When one is with a dying person – or indeed with a newborn child – this is the quality one may touch into. Presence is all. We cut through our conditioned reactions. There is stillness. In therapeutic work, the *brahmaviharas* serve as a compass, something to which we can re-orient when we get lost. We are re-aligning with something deeper. Although these qualities are natural to us, it is also useful – and possible – to cultivate them.

In the training I offer, I ask those present to sit in groups of five. One of the group members sits or lies in the middle. The four people around her/him then each hold the quality of one of the *brahmaviharas*. We do this five times so that each person has a chance to be in the centre and to also experience holding each of the four qualities. It can prove to be a stilling and lovely experience for people, particularly when they are in the centre. Equally, it may be experienced as being quite unspectacular. It doesn't really matter. (It can be useful if, in holding a quality, one does this for oneself as well as for the person in the centre.)

The key aspect is that of resting. More traditional psychotherapy and psychology tend to rely on interpretation, understanding and analysis. I was never drawn to this. It felt like hard work and I didn't really feel smart enough. To be able to rest in the *brahmaviharas* and work from this sense of spaciousness, means everything to me. I work without a sense of an agenda and with the trust that that which needs to arise in the session will do so and that the client and I are in the hands of a wider intelligence. It is pleasant to rest in this. (Which does not mean there isn't a certain 'stretch' often in doing the work. You're not just hanging about.)

Reflection:

What is your first response to reading of the *brahmaviharas*? Do you perhaps have a reaction against them if they do not form part of the faith tradition with which you are familiar? Do you want to explore what might happen if you opened, even for a moment, to this teaching?

The *brahmaviharas* continued

So the *brahmaviharas* or divine abidings – or qualities worth cultivating – are:

Metta – loving kindness

Karuna – compassion

Uppekha – equanimity

Mudita – sympathetic joy

Let me re-state that these qualities are within us. They are our birth right. And they are also 'without' us – and so are qualities that we can rest in. They're not qualities we need to 'crank up'. They are present. We rest in them.

Let me try my best to describe them here.

Metta – loving kindness. This is sometimes described as having a quality of welcome. It is as if someone arrives at your door and you warmly welcome them in.

Karuna – compassion. The person has been kindly welcomed in. We settle together and enter with them into the fullness of their experience. This isn't about detachment. It certainly includes being impacted by the person. There is the 'feeling with' quality that people sometimes describe as compassion. But we don't get lost in the compassion. I will speak of this in a subsequent section.

Uppekha – equanimity. Everything is welcome here. Joy. Silliness. Sexiness. Hilarity. Despair. Absent-ness. The sense of being out of one's body. It is all equally welcome

Mudita – sympathetic joy. This is sometimes described as a note sounding on a stringed instrument and the same note echoing on the instrument alongside it. This is a very precious quality. It offers a huge contribution to the field of psychotherapy – and indeed to any of the healing and caring professions and life in general. Resonating with the joy of the other. I miss this when it's not forthcoming from the person I go to for therapy, as in the following example.

Susan: We were all standing around my uncle's deathbed. He'd probably been dead less than an hour. The bed was next to the huge bay window in his bedroom, overlooking the garden which was a little shabby now from neglect. The carers were there, the hospice nurse, some cousins, me and my two siblings who are his closest nieces and nephews and some of their children. About 16 in all maybe. Also Elizabeth, my beloved friend from England. It felt as if something needed to happen to mark the moment. 'Shouldn't we say a prayer?' I asked tentatively. There was quiet assent and the task seemed to fall to me. We were a room full of various faiths and none. *How does one pull this off?* I wondered. (My uncle himself was of no particular faith.) Whatever I said was heartfelt but it also felt as though everyone in the room was able to make it their own – that is, it didn't offend them. This felt precious. And as though – in the wake of all the pain and confusion precipitated by his illness and death – I had made my particular contribution, and we were together.

I relate this to Van, my therapist. He looks at me with a severe face. He doesn't get it. He doesn't get that this was an important and healing moment. He doesn't share my joy. And I feel sad.

Mudita includes welcoming humour in the therapeutic space. Definitely one of my favourite times with my therapist is when we chuckle or laugh together. It's the time when I am able to feel his humanity more and that he's not on a trip of being a therapist (as I told him just the other day!). Normalcy is good in the therapeutic space.

In holding the *brahmaviharas*, one works with an intention. This is important here and in the work in general. As intention is just that. I *intend* to hold *mudita* – sympathetic joy. An intention is that to which you want to give energy. It orients you in quite a powerful way. In the exercise I have mentioned in the group of five, the invitation is to be with the particular quality one chooses for a period of three minutes. You will not be able to be with the quality for the whole of this period, and indeed may hardly be able to be with it at all. But there is a power in intention. I think you'll find this true if you experiment with it. The frame of mind you bring to something has a subtle but profound impact. Perhaps it's like pausing for grace before a meal or asking for permission before you enter a forest or wild space. It can colour your experience of the particular event.

Ian Rees, a psychotherapist and former trainer at the Karuna Institute, speaks of the *brahmaviharas* being:

... gestures of intention which balance the heart and enable the setting up of a field of relationship which is coherent and balanced... The establishing of this balanced and transformative field is one of the primary tasks of the Core Process Psychotherapist and this teaching therefore is of importance throughout the training and throughout clinical practice.[28]

We can't meet another's suffering or indeed their joy if it comes only from our conditioned selves. We are invited to rest in something bigger than the two of us. There is help. We don't have to be here alone. We rest in a wider field of compassionate intelligence that is not separate from us. This makes all the difference.

Reflection:

Is there one of the *brahmaviharas* that attracts you? If you are not drawn to them, are there other supportive frameworks that you use? If not, how might you establish such holding for yourself – should you indeed wish to do so?

On your own, or with a friend, focus on one of these qualities at a time. You could both hold the same quality for a short time or take turns holding different qualities for each other. Two minutes will be long enough. Just having the intention to hold/rest in the quality is enough. You probably won't notice anything in particular. That's fine. Do this with each of the qualities. Do it regularly, ideally with the support of someone else. (Remember whatever quality you are holding, to hold it for yourself also.)

Can you think of times when someone has resonated with your joy or good fortune? Did you notice how lovely that is? Is this a quality you have been able to offer another?

What is psychotherapy anyway?

You may well ask. As Sean my supervisor says, any word that starts with *psych* is bound to cause people to be a bit nervous.

Basically psychotherapy – the word *psyche* means soul in Greek, which I like – is a commitment to meet with another person, sometimes over quite a long period of time. Typically one would meet for an hour or 50 minutes. It would be formal in the sense that ideally one wouldn't be seeing the person in any other context (for example, socially) and the sessions take on a certain regularity and potency – you might say almost a ritual quality.

Most of us are not fully met when we first need to be – as little ones – and have suffered from a lack of attunement in our early life. Because of the circumstances in which our caregivers found themselves – either within themselves or perhaps with their situation being challenging – they were not always able to give the infants in their care the appropriate loving attention. The infant is finely

Presence in Relationship

tuned and cannot live without affection. This can sound simplistic but it's true – the infant dies without attuned affection and response.[29]

While we may not *literally* die, we may experience much of our life from a sort of frozen state, with a sense of fear or with other sorts of afflictions. Psychotherapy can be an experience akin to being parented again. I remember hearing early in my training that as our wounding happens in relationship, so too is this where our healing lies. This stays with me somehow. And I know not everyone would agree with it. (Most statements – whoever makes them – aren't eternally true for everyone at all times.)

A friend Glen recently expressed to me the sense of shame that prevents him from considering going into longer term therapy. For him, this step would remind him of his woundedness. Yes, it can unfortunately feel shameful.

I explained to him that my view of therapy is different from this. It can actually be excellent to be in therapy when one feels in a less vulnerable position. That is, I don't make a necessary correlation between being in an awful space and seeking therapy. Perhaps I say this also as I was in therapy as a requirement for the Core Process training – which lasted seven years. Seeing a therapist when one is in a relatively robust state can be useful in that all one's energy isn't going into managing a crisis. This can enable one to enquire into one's life from a wider perspective rather than narrowly focusing on one particular area of concern. Glen seemed surprised by this and comforted by the thought that seeing a therapist need not be regarded as a sign of weakness.

Similarly I regard it as excellent not to quit therapy at the first signs of improvement. It is so lovely to have someone alongside delighting with you when things are going well. And it takes time to integrate the good changes that happen. This can be quite a challenge and is a theme I will return to later.

Maura suggests that those who are perhaps in the most danger are those of us walking around without any mental health diagnosis.[30] We can so easily slip into thinking we are the ones who are okay. Well, the good news – I think it's good – is that there's no *us* and *them* in this. Maybe the fundamental arrogance is around mental health. Yes, it may be that those of us who have not (yet) been attended to by friends or the medical profession for psychological care, are in the most need of help. It seems pretty evident to me that those practising psychiatry and psychology may be particularly wounded. I don't regard this as a bad thing. Rather, I feel it can allow for great compassion and sensitivity to others in difficulty. I have had several clients who are either psychologists or psychiatrists, and life is tough for them. They can tend to know too much and feel they have an understanding of their own 'story'. This can be rather unhelpful.

I remember requesting a few sessions of counselling – quite a few years ago – when I was aware I was about to make a rather dangerous life manoeuvre and thought to get a counsellor on board so that she could also be with me in the aftermath to this. (Happily I don't think I needed to return to her.) This I would call the emergency model of counselling or therapy. And it was helpful.

Longer term therapy is of quite a different order. There is the opportunity for profound change and transformation. Including the body and having a sense of the spiritual or the wider holding field, gives breadth and depth to the work. It is a great offering to another if one is able to go to subtle body/mind territory with them as this is sometimes the level at which healing needs to occur – in the territory of early wounding before language.

And we must, I think, guard against thinking we are trying to iron out all the deliciously human quirks – in ourselves and others. This would be a real pity. Perhaps delighting in each other's funny stuff – and yes, our own mostly – is the way to go. There can be a danger in any healing form to want to get rid of what is messy and imperfect. That's not the deal!

Re-reading some of the Swiss psychiatrist Carl Jung's work, I am reminded of his movement away from looking at pathology and illness towards exploring what helps human beings really flourish.[31] Can you feel your back straightening and yourself smiling as you read this? This is a helpful emphasis – at least for those of us who are lucky enough not to be in immediate crisis. Perhaps we can experience life more fully and more delightfully. This is what the spiritual traditions are on about. And psychotherapy can support this.

I know people who attend therapy weekly over years as an ongoing spiritual practice.[32] It's a way of keeping current with yourself. For the vulnerable, it's a way of maintaining health, managing life, work and parenting. For the slightly more robust, it can hugely enrich your life.

Maura speaks of all of life being a return journey.[33] The work, she says, is to bring us back into human kindness and relationship.[34] 'Awakening into contact' is a phrase Maura uses of Core Process Psychotherapy. She wisely asserts that it's preferable to be less enlightened and in relationship with other human beings than to be enlightened but unable to be in such contact.[35]

But perhaps nothing answers the question 'what is psychotherapy?' better than the title of the paper of Maura's that I have already referred to: *Psychotherapy as a spiritual journey*. This is what it is.

Reflection:

Do you sense any pull towards the sort of skilful, loving attention that can be offered in the psychotherapeutic relationship? Is this something you would ever consider pursuing? What might hold you back from this?

Some reflections on Buddhism in the West

I was struck – as it so resonated for me – when one of my tutors said that Buddhism was not suited to the western psyche.[36] As far as I am aware, there is not much spoken about this though I gather CG Jung, while valuing practices from the East, warned his western students of the dangers of practicing these.[37]

I would not be where I am today were it not for the Buddhist tradition. And on my shelves you will find just as many treasures from this tradition as from Christianity. Indeed, I move between the two without a sense of there being any boundary between them.

What might my tutor have meant when she said what she did? Our society today is very different from that which the Buddha – and indeed Jesus – inhabited. Both of these teachers taught mostly outdoors and a sense of interconnection was much more the lived experience of the people they were addressing than is the case with most of us today. In a talk given on retreat at Gaia House in the south of England, Maura spoke of how the Buddha's teaching was perfect for his time.[38] There was a sense of connectedness in the society in which there was subsistence living, with people living close to the land. The Buddha thus didn't have to teach about this.

We live in a very individualistic age. For many of us, our experience of ourselves is as isolated human beings.[39] The Buddhist meditation practice is typically quite rigorous. On a retreat or at an evening's meditation, one may be encouraged to sit on a cushion on the floor – generally without back support – for a period of about 40 minutes. In a retreat setting, one may easily do this four times a day. There is often instruction about following the breath, watching your thinking... that sort of thing. This can be pretty hard going.

Such practices need to be undertaken with care and may not always be helpful. There was a time when I felt that I should stop this form of practice and thankfully I did so. I was finding I was experiencing isolation – though I was among many other people. I was 'watching' myself in a way that made my gaze on myself too clinical and this was becoming unhelpful. My experience of my life was already one of being isolated so this did not feel useful for me. The practice draws many people who are already quite introverted and can result in them feeling that it's okay to be out of touch with others. (Remember I speak from experience!)

Many seeking a spiritual path are attracted to Buddhism as the Christian church has not met their needs. For me, a huge value of Buddhism was that I didn't have to bother about God language. God has become quite contested territory! We all seem to mean different things when we speak of her.

It may be a question of instruction. Sitting silently in a group can prove to be profoundly transformative. In my first experience of this – in a group of about five women who sat quietly in an ordinary lounge on ordinary chairs in a small town in South Africa – it was as if my psyche was being rearranged. It was curious. There was then no instruction as to what we were doing. I think the period was about 25 minutes at the most (once a week).

I also want to acknowledge that different practices – and no practice – are useful at different times in one's life. And then it is the courage to move on that is important. And perhaps then the challenge is not to trash the tradition one is moving away from. Each has its place. And perhaps in moving away, one is fulfilling the tradition in a more profound way than if one stayed.

Some of the most beautiful books I return to time after time are from the Buddhist tradition. And some of the talks I have most loved are from this tradition. I think of Rob Burbea at Sharpham in the south of England, moving so easily between Christianity and Buddhism. I think of one of the Ajahns I heard speak at Sharpham – he was the abbot of one of the monasteries in England. Before his talk, we were to sit for 30 minutes. In preparation for this, everyone got their backs straight and became serious. The Ajahn simply looked around smiling. And continued to do this as the 'sitting' started. There was no time when you could say he went from 'not meditation' to 'meditation'. I suppose this is what Paul in the Bible means when he says 'pray always'. I just watched the Ajahn and found this a most rewarding experience. Clearly Buddhism was working for him. And these days, many teachers would acknowledge that the very word meditation is tricky.

Much of the Buddhist practice is about practising compassion, and yet clearly this is not easy for many of us.[40] Several people have told me that they find the practice of *metta* – loving kindness – very difficult.[41] Perhaps the teaching of Christianity on love is more accessible.

Buddhism is essentially, I feel, a very advanced teaching. Tradition tells us that the Buddha did not intend to teach as he assumed that he would not be understood.[42] I think mostly we do not understand the teaching at all. It is only after living a lot and undergoing experience in psychotherapy that I am able to experience (something of) what he taught. And then, as some would say, when you've got the message, hang up the phone. In the Buddhist tradition, it's said that you use a raft to get to the other side of the river. But once you've got there, don't lug the raft around with you.

Reflection:

Do you have any response to what is written here?

If you have experience – directly – of Buddhism, does any of this resonate for you? Or perhaps you differ sharply from this?

For some people the very word Buddhism is

problematic. If this is so for you, can you just breathe with this? Could you talk to someone about it?

Reflections on western Buddhism continued

'Bring the mind back home.' This might be a kind and wise meditation instruction. I feel, however, that we need to include the body far more. What about: bring the body back home. Can you feel how the very phrase shifts something in you, bringing you closer to the ground? The western affliction is to think the mind is king. Below the neck gets hardly a look in. There will be no health among us until this changes.

The helpful and sometimes hilarious Pema Chodron in *When Things Fall Apart*, speaks of how Trungpa Rinpoche progressively changed his teaching in the West.[43] He was realising that people from this culture responded unhelpfully to teaching that would not have caused difficulty in the East. So he learnt not to use the word 'concentrate'. This word would cause people to sort of scrunch up their faces and try too hard. Instead, he began to say that about 25 percent of the attention should be on the breath. Pema gives various examples of how Trungpa lovingly and wisely changed how he phrased the teachings. It is hard to teach people in the West. We get so serious! Many of us are so off God that we are quite reactive to any mention of the divine. I find – happily it's changing – one can be nervous of speaking of Buddhism in a Christian gathering and dare not mention God in a Buddhist one. This separation is unhelpful.

A client of mine, who follows Buddhist practice with devotion and commitment, had a sort of waking dream of being held by the Buddha and Christ. This, although in her 'real life' she has not the least interest and certainly no 'belief' in Christ. To me this suggests at a profound – that is, beyond the cognitive – level the non-separation of what the Buddha and Christ represent.

Some writers have argued that bringing Buddhism and Christianity together will be a central task of our time.

It's beautiful when we allow silence to happen naturally. Do you notice how when we try to be quiet, somehow we can lose contact with each other and become a bit self-conscious about the 'project' of silence? Rowan Williams, formerly archbishop of Canterbury, shares how some of the work that he loved best was being with children in the lower grades in school and suggesting they all sit together quietly. This, the children just did – no big deal – and thoroughly enjoyed. Oh, we make spirituality into such a project. I know because I did it, and probably still do to some degree.

Maura makes a good point when she says that our spiritual practice may lull us into complacency – as, she adds, can psychotherapy.[44] She speaks of how the way we practice Buddhism can cause more suffering.[45] In the West, she says, we have difficulty orienting to health, goodness and well-being[46]. It is sad that this is so but this is my experience of myself and my clients.

I certainly affirm that Buddhist practice, in the sense of regular meditation and reading, can save a life. I think of a client Arthur who has experienced unmitigated suffering in his life. The last five years or so of practice, following tapes and readings and regularly sitting still on a cushion for between two and four hours a day, have enabled him to get some kind of hold on his life. It would be an interesting study – that I so hope he will write one day – to look at how the practice he does on his cushion and meeting with me differ and yet inform each other.

I recall the well-known Buddhist teacher Thanissara, who was responsible for introducing the Core Process foundation training in South Africa, saying that despite years of meditation, there were certain states such as depression that meditation alone could not shift for her.[47]

I remember my therapist in England, when I said I was feeling isolated, suggesting I get on the phone to as many people as possible. Break the isolation, was what she was saying. I'm mentioning this here as one could consider the Buddhist teaching to be saying: whatever your condition, sit with it. Suffer it out. Well, it may be saying that (I'm not sure it is) but I'm saying that's not always the best idea. Taking action to remedy the situation can be far kinder.

In *Buddhism Without Beliefs*, Stephen Batchelor emphasises that the Buddha taught practices rather than starting a religion:[48]

> Instead of presenting himself as a saviour, the Buddha saw himself as a healer. [49]

Jesus, too saw himself in this way. As perhaps did the founders of other great spiritual traditions.

Many of these talk of The Way. Perhaps in our time, Core Process is a form useful for healing.

Reflection:

Do you appreciate periods of quietness? Is it something you could include more deliberately in your life?

Applied Buddhism

Somebody has referred to Core Process Psychotherapy as applied Buddhism. I think one could put it that way. Maura has called psycho-therapy a post-meditation practice.[50] This feels helpful.

Chodron – whose book *When Things Fall Apart* I would recommend reading again and again – says of practising meditation:

> We're just being with our experience, whatever it is. If our experience is that sometimes we have some kind of perspective, and sometimes we have none, then that's our experi-ence. If sometimes we can approach what scares us, and sometimes we absolutely can't, then that's our expe-rience... Just seeing what's going on – that's the teaching.[51]

This is beautiful. And it's hard to do on one's own.

In Core Process Psychotherapy it is the practitioner who is holding this intention to 'be with'. 'Just stay with it a bit if you can,' might be what one says to the client.

Batchelor contrasts the term *dharma practice* with the word Buddhism. *Dharma* practice suggests a course of action, he says, whereas Buddhism suggests a belief system.[52] (*Dharma* refers to the teachings of the Buddha as well as to the nature of reality which he was seeking to describe.[53]) Core Process, though it has theoretical underpinnings, is essentially a practice. Some of my colleagues prefer to regard themselves as *dharma* practitioners rather than using the more complicated term psychotherapist. I have sympathy with this view and in this book often use the term practitioner.

For clients who practise meditation, the practice of Core Process Psychotherapy alongside this can be quite interesting. For Jonathan, a practitioner of meditation with a rigorous daily practice, our work was perhaps in part about bridging the divide between this practice and daily life which we both recognised felt worlds apart. As he said: 'I can do the meditation. That's easy. It's the other I just can't handle.' But after about 18 months of working together, we both sensed this distance was lessening.

Seemingly small statements can be evidence of a gentle healing process. Another client, also a committed Buddhist practitioner, who experiences excruciating pain on any meetings with people, on one occasion could say: 'At one point, I wept for my pain.' It is a sign of growth when a person is able to begin to experience compassion for themselves.

Another client said of our sessions: 'There's no conflict between this and my meditation.' The regular work in psychotherapy had transformed his meditation practice.

I think Core Process Psychotherapy as applied Buddhism is perhaps the best use the West can make of the Buddhist tradition today. It is Buddhism in relationship. Too many of us are too good at going it alone. Chodron says of relating compassionately with others:

> There's nothing more advanced than relating with others. There's nothing more advanced than communication – compassionate communication.[54]

For some, the spiritual task may be to find a way of being more fully 'in the world' and in relationship.[55]

Reflection:

Do you get a sense of what I mean by Core Process Psychotherapy as applied Buddhism?

If you practise meditation, how do you experience the relationship between this and everyday life?

Our storyline

I suppose it's good that many of us have become so 'emotionally literate' and can give an articulate account of how we are and why. (Even young people can give you a whole story about their day.) But we need to move beyond this too as we can get so stuck in our own explanations. We use words like 'co-dependency' and 'narcissistic' with ease. But what do we really mean? There are a thousand nuances to these words.

This is where the body is key. But of course it's not as articulate so a different kind of patience and curiosity is needed. But it is so worth it. Let me give two brief examples – one from clinical work and one from a conversation with a friend.

Brent: My body is tired and aching. It's like this after squash and doesn't get to loosen up before I play the next game three days later.

Susan: What about if we uncouple it from the squash and just stay with it as it is now. Perhaps there's some wisdom in this.

The session progresses – I don't now remember how – but we separate Brent's experience in his body from the 'storyline' of it being about squash.

By the end of the session, Brent is baffled. 'It's gone. My body's relaxed. What's going on here?'

For Brent, this may be a turning point in the kind of midlife enquiry in which he is engaged.

The second example:

Carol: After doing house-sitting for 10 days, I can't settle back into my home and routine though I've been back a few days now. I feel thrown somehow.

Susan: What if you separate it from the house-sitting? What if there's just a sense of unsettled-ness? What if you could just be interested in that?

This place Carol's called 'unsettled' then becomes a rather magical place of transition, a place where she's being called to something new. The house-sitting, rather than interrupting something, has formed a break from Carol's usual surroundings and routine and allowed her to look at her life in a new way. Carol is a woman in a profound time of transition.

This 'dropping the storyline' is quite simple and so beautiful. I hope I'm giving you some sense of it here.

Reflection:

Do you relate to this critique of emotional literacy? Do you sense that emotional literacy could have limitations? Or perhaps you don't feel emotionally literate at all.

Is your interest stirred by the two short examples I give of sort of bypassing the storyline? Might you like to try it some time?

Awareness

Awareness. In Core Process Psychotherapy, we rest in the transformative quality of awareness. Just that.

> The particular flavour of Core Process training is very much founded on the transformative nature of awareness.[56]

I was first introduced to the concept of awareness when a friend gave me a book by that name – *Awareness* – by the Jesuit priest Anthony De Mello, who had sadly died by the time his series of talks had been transcribed and put into this book. He speaks of awareness as being delightful.

Let me try to give an example of this from this morning.

It is summer in the southern hemisphere. It's a Saturday. The area is quiet. I leave home for a walk in the neighbourhood. The air is fresh. I feel good walking. After maybe 10 minutes of the 40-minute walk, I begin thinking. How can I earn a bit more? What if I got a friend to run a bed-and-breakfast from my place? What would I need to put in place for this? How much would that cost? A few blocks from home, I think: hey, where've I been? Awareness is delightful. Endless pondering in one's head really isn't that great and invariably comes to nothing. So back we come to the present moment. A few lines I wrote last year come to mind:

> If you take just 10 steps
> knowing your feet meet the earth
> you've lived the day well.

Mindfulness is a word that is being used a lot at present in a huge variety of contexts. Awareness perhaps holds a wider field in the sense that one might limit mindfulness rather to the mind, which would be a pity.

Franklyn Sills speaks of the *Satipattana Sutra* being the original text on mindfulness. *Sati,* he points out, can be translated as presence.

Sometimes the word mindfulness can rather strip the mystery from *sati*. Rees is helpful on this:

> One of the things that struck me
> is the mysterious nature of *sati*

(mindfulness) and that when one initially comes across it, you can pick it up as a technique or even a method but essentially it is a mystery which opens to greater and greater depths as you open to it.[57]

There is a simplicity to *sati*.

De Mello likens awareness to watching the clouds pass in the sky. Rather than identify with a particular cloud, one senses the cloud against the backdrop of the sky and is aware of the changing motion of the clouds in the sky. The clouds here might be states of mind or a sensation in the body: one is aware of this and then it passes and changes. It is relating from a place of openness to life as it happens. It is knowing the essential emptiness of things. (This is a topic I return to later.) To quote Rees again:

The experience of the inherently liberating nature of awareness is... central to the practice of Core Process Psychotherapy.[58]

Franklyn has said: '*Sati*, or presence, is the core of the work we do.'[59] He continues:

Sati has the connotation of a state of presence, an open, wide and soft perceptual field that can hold whatever arises and passes in perceptual awareness.

One of Franklyn's colleagues, Laura Donington, puts it this way in her helpful article entitled *Core Process Psychotherapy*:

In Core Process awareness in the present is seen as inherently integrative and healing.[60]

Most of us develop a rather fixed sense of ourselves. Awareness allows more of a sense of movement as we become interested and curious about who we are.

In *Licking Honey from the Razor's Edge*, Maura speaks of awareness in this way:

Any psychotherapy that is about experience and about direct enquiry through awareness has got... to move beyond concepts. [There] is a challenge to become aware of the actual moment of experience, not just conceptually but experientially, at subtle and more complex levels.[61]

And:

What makes a Buddhist psychotherapy practitioner different from other practitioners is intentionality. When one is working through enquiry into the nature of how things are in the moment there has to be an intention to be aware. This means just allowing awareness – full stop.[62]

She goes on to say that we know from sitting in meditation how much effort this actually takes![63] I am not assuming you, the reader, understand what I mean by the term 'awareness'. It can be a whole new language and experience when you first come across it. It was for me. Perhaps suffice to say at this point is that for the practitioner it means restraining oneself – not interpreting, giving clever responses or even asking smart questions. The emphasis in Core Process Psychotherapy is being present with the person and noticing what arises – in yourself and in the field with the person. I will be saying a lot more about this.

Reflection:

Do you have a sense of what I'm talking about
when I speak of awareness? If not, can you let go
of any sense of inadequacy that might come up
for you around this? Curiosity is enough.

A session

Andrew is a man who had been close to death due to an obscure liver condition.

It's the last week of January. Andrew arrives for his appointment. He's smart in a white shirt with brown stripes, trousers and boots. 'You look cool and relaxed,' he says to me. He slowly and carefully folds the shirtsleeves up to his elbows.

Andrew: It's a perfect time to see you.

Susan: Good.

Andrew: Well... [uncertain] You know I said I'd be getting that contract. (Andrew is moving from a senior position in the health industry to being a consultant.) Well, it arrived late yesterday and I only opened it this morning. I'm furious. (He gave some details about the contract here.) I feel like lashing out. I'm bitterly disappointed.

After a little while.

Susan: How is your body doing now that you've told me this?

Andrew: I feel something here. [Indicating his chest area but somehow giving me the sense — from his gesture — that he's referring to the area just outside his body, above his chest.]

Susan: [gesturing] So it's the area here, on top of your chest?

Andrew: Yes.

Susan: As though there's pressure on your chest?

Andrew: Yes, that's right.

A little later.

Andrew: There's something else. [Long pause.]

I sense this is difficult for Andrew to say.

Andrew: I've been waking up at four o'clock — I check the time and it's always four — with my heart beating and I feel such fear. The one time my nose was very slightly blocked. I've decided to get up when that happens and I go and sit in the lounge. It reminds me of the time earlier last year when I was so aware of my mortality. I become afraid I won't be able to breathe.

Susan: [After some further conversation] What do you do when you get up?

Andrew: The one time I listened to music. Another time I read.

Susan: That's good Andrew. I was hoping you didn't get down to doing e-mails or something like that.

Andrew: No.

Some silence.

Susan: Yes, I was up in the night last night. A cat was crying outside. And I was somehow struck by how beautiful the night was.

Andrew: Yes, I opened the lounge curtains. I'd disabled the alarm in that part of the house but not the whole house so I didn't go outside but as I opened them, I was struck by how beautiful it was.

Susan: Oh. Was it the darkness or what?

Presence in Relationship

Andrew: Well, I was so struck that it was nearly dawn. That surprised me.

Susan: [Some time later] ...Well, one can't help being a bit metaphorical about that. You felt dawn was closer than you'd thought.

Here I am alluding to the transition period of Andrew leaving full-time employment to be a part-time consultant. He is now 55 and has known, since his youth, that this is the age at which he should retire from salaried work. Yet he feels unable to take that step fully at present, also given that he has family members he is supporting financially. As his therapist I am aware of several very interesting projects that beckon and where I sense there is a lot of energy in Andrew, though perhaps it would mean a few months with less or no money.

Andrew is stretching back in his chair. His head is back in a sort of an arch.

Susan: How is that position for you?

Andrew: I like it.

Susan: So your neck doesn't need support?

Andrew: No, somehow this position forms a good spot between my head and my neck and it makes me feel quite strong.

Susan: Oh, that's great. (I was surprised as when I tried to mimic the position, I didn't find it at all comfortable.)

I become aware of a sort of tingling in my legs at several points in the session. I just notice this and at times, it prompts me to ask Andrew how his body is doing.

Susan: How is your body doing now?

Andrew: Well. It feels something's loosened up.

Susan: Yes. I feel some tingling in my legs.

For me, these body sensations are a possible indication of aliveness and energy in Andrew's life.

But I don't need to articulate that. I just notice the sensations and let them go.

Later in the session.

Andrew: I think waking at four must be to do with the contract – that I was anxious about that.

Susan: Yes, that was my first thought too. But then I wondered whether you are perhaps digesting again your experience of the first half of last year (when he had been close to death.) We've spoken about the fact that anniversaries of significant medical dates are coming up soon.

Andrew: Yes, the 27 February is really when things got so serious

Susan: Okay, that was my sense. Though you say that the condition began the August before, but the acute danger was in February.

(We are meeting towards the end of January.)

Andrew: My cousin and I were going out for a

coaching session. I didn't know where to go. Then I found myself heading for S (a local church and retreat centre). I hadn't been there for years. I would go there as a boy for retreats. (Andrew had never mentioned this before.)

Susan: For retreats? Were you at a Catholic school?

Andrew: Yes, a Catholic boys school.

Susan: Who led the retreats?

Andrew: A more senior boy. He went on to become a priest in that order.

Susan: Gee, how marvellous. A retreat led by a boy. How many of you would there be?

Andrew: About 12.

I feel interested in this rather forgotten aspect of Andrew's life.

A pause.

Andrew: We used to go to church – as a family. I was more traditional than my wife. I went past Sacred Heart on my way home the other day and felt quite a pull to it. (This is a reference to a local church.)

Another pause.

Susan: Hmm, maybe you could attend there now and again.

My sense is that this early experience was formative for Andrew and perhaps needed reclaiming in some way.

Andrew: We headed for the chapel. I said to my cousin: let's just sit quietly and gather our thoughts. To my surprise, when I opened my eyes, we'd sat for 10 minutes. Then we went out into the grounds and found a bench and spent an hour and a half there. It was lovely.

And again I sense that revisiting this particular space – the environment that was so meaningful to Andrew in his youth – is significant.

In response to the suggestion from me Andrew acknowledges that yes, maybe he could visit the centre now and again.

Andrew: I would like to be more in tune.

Susan: What do you mean by that?

Andrew: Sort of know more how I am at the time.

Susan: It's a nice musical way of putting it.

Andrew: I love music though I don't play an instrument. I'm always listening to music.

I think we were talking here about the value of sensing into the body. This seems to be of huge value to Andrew and at this stage he needs support in noticing this.

Susan: You're welcome to stand up and move in the room if you want to.

Andrew: Another time.

Susan: If you were to move, what would you be doing?

(In myself I had a sense of wanting to stand, to move.)

Andrew: I'd be pacing.

Susan: Oh. What kind of strides would you be making? Would you be just in this room or would they extend outside? (I'd imagined maybe long angry strides.)

Andrew: No, they'd be slow strides. I'd be thinking.

Before Andrew leaves...

Susan: It's been a full session. How will you handle the rest of the day?

Andrew: This afternoon I'm meeting with two friends.

Susan: And this morning? Could you do some walking, some pacing? Stay a bit with the impact this morning has had?

Andrew: Yes, I could try and do that.

He stands to leave.

Susan: I feel you're on the right track... though it may not be a track you're liking at present.

I say this as I know this is a bit of a tough time for Andrew.

Reflection:

What is your sense of this account of the session with Andrew? Does it leave you uncomfortable? Curious?

Is there any particular detail that strikes you or reminds you of something in yourself or in your own body?

PART
2

Emptiness

Emptiness is close to the quality of *sati* – presence – that was introduced in the previous section. In part 2 we look in more detail at how this quality can be held with another therapeutically and in everyday relationship. It is close to spaciousness but perhaps a little different too. Some may refer to it as the unconditioned or the unborn. For many, this would be what they would call God. (In one of his Lenten writings, Laurence Freeman talks of God as the emptiness which is fullness.[64]) This is the territory of the *brahmaviharas* without which depth healing cannot happen.

A significant text here are words from the *Heart Sutta*, one of the discourses attributed to the Buddha, Siddhartha Gautama. When I enquired as to why this is called the *Heart Sutta,*[65] I was told: well, this is the heart of the matter.

> Form is emptiness; emptiness is form.
> Emptiness is not other than form;
> form is not other than emptiness.

This is a weighty saying and not easy to understand.

It has taken me years to value it and it still changes shape for me, as it were. It can be good to dwell on just the first two phrases – form is emptiness; emptiness is form. As I understand it – and there would have been tomes written on this – at least in part it is saying that there is no divide between what we call the material and the spiritual.

There is something about this territory of emptiness that can be frightening and we can want to flee it at all costs. And we all do. Yet sometimes we're almost forced to just be there with nothing going on, no one to see – maybe even an electricity blackout and we can't use the computer. (With our electronic world, we can pretty much dodge this space much of the time.) I was amused to notice that the word 'void' is contained in the word 'avoid'. I see how I can try to avoid what I anticipate will be an experience of void. And if I just can't do that for some reason, it can turn out to be such a blessing. It is as if finally my soul finds a place to land. As if there's a great sigh. At last. *Why did I try to flee from this?* I ask myself.

There's a phrase in Buddhism – and no doubt it's used more widely – 'empty mind'. This is sometimes referred to as beginner's mind. It's rather beautiful. I don't know whether you can catch the scent of it. You don't have to be smart. You can just be interested or curious. You can just show up. You allow emptiness and an interest in whatever is in front of you – be that a feeling in yourself, the person opposite you, whatever... Our knowledge can clutter things up. Feeling we know something does give a sense of security but also blocks other possibilities and ways of knowing.

I am emphasising emptiness rather than form here. It is this that is neglected in western culture. Yet I was challenged by a colleague recently who said of the *Heart Sutta*, that while form and emptiness are said to be equal, Buddhists seem to privilege emptiness. I feel this is an accurate observation. I suppose most of us are drawn to one of these po-larities – which I'm suggesting aren't polarities at all. Many of those who prioritise a spiritual path, particularly those of a Buddhist-type inclination, may spend a lot of time on retreat and in silence and somewhat flee from the messiness of contact with other human beings. Someone said that we choose our religion to suit our neurosis. Maybe. I think I have done that. The invitation is to be with form or emptiness and know that they are not separate from one another. It is the intriguing journey of a lifetime.

Reflection:

Which do you feel you emphasise more in your life – form or emptiness? Are you interested in giving more attention to the other of the pair? How might you do this?

Do you relate to what I say about the void? Have you had the experience of not being able to dodge the void and it turns out to be an experience of richness?

Form and emptiness in Core Process Psychotherapy

I can tend to assume that people know what I mean when I speak of form (and then I discover that they don't). I refer here to that which is more formed. The human body is a form. So too are feelings. The family meal is a form. Forms can be intentionally created and be part of tradition or culture. I hope this begins to give you a sense of form.

A lovely challenge of our time is, as I wrote in my journal not long ago, to

create forms where p/Presence is known.[66]

Core Process Psychotherapy is one such form. The framework is that we meet for an hour and typically language is used. That is the form. And at every moment there is also emptiness. It is in this that the work rests. You might call it the un-conditioned. So every moment has an openness, a porousness to it. You can experience that.

So one begins each session with a client from a state of spaciousness or emptiness, as if beginning with a blank canvas – even if one has met with the person many times before. And this spaciousness is present too throughout the session. And yet form is there too. One is not sitting in a spaciousness that does not include contact, connection and being impacted by the person.

Some of us who are comfortable in 'spiritual' territory can be over-spacious and as a result people may not feel a sense of connection with us. We have become disembodied in a way. In Core Process Psychotherapy we are holding the emptiness but within form.

Let me say a little more on emptiness here. You might see it as a positive sense of space. You could image it as a wide landscape – uncluttered and beautiful. It can be seen as womb-like, a space of potential, perhaps with a sense of expectancy to it. And yet the spaciousness itself is of value; it is not just a space waiting to be filled. It can be linked to a sense of ground – and indeed a sense of being grounded is essential to the work – for the practitioner. There is a certain relaxed alertness. Another way to explain this is that one does not have an agenda. One arrives with empty hands and, in a sense, remains with empty hands throughout the session. No being the expert here. Simply resting in compassionate awareness and being impacted by the other.

It can be a lovely sign of health if more space/emptiness appears in the therapeutic session. I think of Jennifer. Sessions with her are full. She has much to share from what is happening in her life. After a couple of years, a sense of there being more 'room' emerges in the sessions. We may sit quietly for a few seconds. This is new. It's early days but it's lovely to notice and I remark on it. 'Yes, I feel less tortured,' she responds.

Reflection:

How do you relate to the encouragement to allow emptiness within relationship? Is there a way you could experiment with this? How would you do so?

Suffering can be known/a knowing arises

There is a knowing that arises. This is something Franklyn says often. And I can say with sureness, certainly of the therapeutic space, that yes, there is a knowing that arises.

The nature of this knowing is perhaps rather unusual. It's more that you get a whiff of something and that you pay attention to this. So sitting with my friend Carin earlier today, she told me about the 'crash', as she put it, that she had experienced the previous day. She described this as huge worry about the future and what would become of her. As she spoke, I experienced a slight prickle behind my eyes, which prompted me to ask: 'Do you feel you need to have a good cry about it?' 'No,' she said, but within moments I needed to leave the room to fetch tissues as she wept freely, telling me how in her childhood she had moved 17 times in 11 years. That is the nature of the knowing. Catching something somehow, even before it is manifest in the space. In working with a client in Core Process, one stays close to this (ever-changing) territory.

The knowing I am speaking of is without an emphasis on the analysis that is found in many forms of psychotherapy. It is more a direct experiential knowing. It involves letting the information come to you rather than grabbing after it. As Franklyn says, no force is needed.[67]

So although I didn't have details about Carin's life I could pick up what was in the field. You may have experienced this way of knowing from the sixth sense that lets you know a loved one is in difficulty even if they're far away from you. This natural skill can be developed.

Franklyn often speaks of the knowing which arises naturally when a settled field is established, supported by the *brahmaviharas* and resting in a wider intelligence. There is nothing magical about this – although at a certain level, yes, it *is* magical. It's simply letting the forces of life do their work.[68]

> *Sati* has the connotation of a state of presence, an open, wide and soft perceptual field that can hold whatever arises and passes in perceptual awareness. The state of *sati* leads to

a state of knowing ...It is about entering a state of awareness within which
knowing arises.[69]

The Bushman Winter has Come is a wonderful
book by Paul Myburgh who relates his seven-year
stay with the San people of the Kalahari. Here you
read of the world of knowing where spirit and
earth are one. The San people occupy fully both of
these realms. They sense an animal in their bodies when out hunting. There is deeply embodied
knowing. This is the nature of the knowing that
arises in Core Process. And it is not far from us.
We can learn to attend to the other in a way that
allows this natural knowing to arise. Franklyn says,
'It is as though you know the client's thoughts and
feelings as they arise in the relational field.'[70] I can
certainly attest to that.

I have spoken about how Maura regards Core
Process Psychotherapy as a two-person meditation practice and of the second ennobling truth
– suffering can be known. Psychotherapy offers
something different here from solitary meditation
in that it is knowing suffering (and other experiences) *with another* that is key. I'm not sure that
too much trying to sit with suffering on one's own
is necessarily good for us.

Our life asks to be attended to. I will go on to discuss the quality of the attention that is offered in the therapeutic space that allows this kind of knowing to arise.

Reflection:

Is there anything here about 'knowing' that is familiar to you? Do you have examples of this from your own life?

Is there someone from whom, when you're with them, you can sense this level of knowing? Is this something you value?

Paying attention

Often we don't welcome the injunction to 'pay attention'. But what kind of attention are we talking about here?

Franklyn writes on the theme of offering another attention. We have been trained to give attention in a way that narrows our gaze and fixes on the object of our attention rather than developing a perceptual field which takes in the whole.[71] When we're sitting with another, this can mean that we over-focus on them, literally or metaphorically leaning towards them and losing our own sense of ground. This is usually unhelpful both for the practitioner and the client.

One starts with giving attention to being grounded and settled in one's own body. I offer a short exercise on this in my training programme. Seated on the floor on a chair with a supportive backrest, I invite the group to imagine a midline from the crown of their head to their sitting bones/pelvis. They can either sense or imagine this line. They then imagine this line continuing from their pelvis into the ground, as though they are being held by a strong root. I refer to this as resting in your fulcrum. A fulcrum is your strong balanced point.[72] For some, imagining the midline extending up from the crown of the head is also helpful. My sense is that for most of us it's the downward movement that is key. Perhaps even as you read this you get a sense of the grounded-ness that it brings.

We then move into a simple exercise designed to practice holding what I call a soft focus. I often give the example of looking at the moon. When the moon catches our attention in the night sky, we often have a sense of it as a whole – there is the moon in the sky, surrounded by the dark, perhaps with clouds racing by. It is in its context and that is part of its beauty. So with the person in front of us. We take in their whole form. We don't just fix on their face though it may seem that our gaze is there. We take in their form and, as it were, the space around them. So one has a sense of using peripheral vision, having a wide focus, soft eyes.[73]

In pairs, I outline this exercise: Be sure you're both comfortable with the space between you. Some people need quite a bit of space between themselves and the other person, so take your time getting this right. Even moving just a centimetre can be important.

You'll take turns playing the role of client and of therapist. If you are the client, you can have your eyes open or closed and you can just be with whatever your experience is. There is nothing you have to do.

If you are the therapist, your eyes are open. You attend to the person in front of you, but from a wide perspective, from this soft focus, taking in the entirety of the person in front of you and the space around them.

Before we begin the exercise, I talk the group through the fulcrum exercise so that everyone begins from a grounded place.

We do this for two minutes and then the pair changes roles.

The follow-up exercise is what I call the 50/50 exercise.

If you are the client, the instructions here are the same. Your eyes are open or closed, and you are just there – there is nothing you need to do.

As therapist, your eyes are open, and the intention is to give 50 percent of your attention to yourself and 50 percent to the person in front of you. It's a bit like rubbing your tummy and patting your head at the same time.

Again, this exercise is done for two minutes. (We do the grounding practice before each of the exercises.)

After both exercises are complete, the pair share with each other their experience of doing this piece of work. Often people break into giggles at this point! I was once doing an evening presentation just outside the city where I live and a woman had to leave the room and laugh uproariously under the night sky for quite a while before she could return. It was rather lovely.

If there is an uneven number of people in the room, I do the exercise with the group so that each person is in a pair. I am often aware of the increased sense of safety I feel when the therapist in the exercise is giving herself attention as well as giving this to me (in the 50/50 exercise). There's something about knowing the therapist is taking care of herself that is re-assuring.

Perhaps a few more words on the 50/50 practice. There's no *right* way to do this. You may be able to hold the balance of attention in this way – attending equally to yourself and to the person in front of you. Or all your attention may be on yourself for a while and then all of it may go to the other person. People find their individual way with this. And again it's attention in the sense of light awareness.

Reflection:

Find a willing friend or family member and try these exercises out, with the person who is playing the role of therapist keeping the time – or set a timer. Keep to just two minutes each way. Begin with the grounding exercise each time.

Share your experience with each other. What was difficult? What was enjoyable? Do you sense any wisdom in holding the wide focus and the 50/50? How might you practice this further?

Brilliant sanity

The paradigm you use makes all the difference. I go to my naturopath and come away feeling so well. I go to a conventional general practitioner (GP) and come away upset, distressed – not trusting my body. It seems to boil down to whether the model is one of health or disease. You see what you are looking for.[74]

The non-traumatised baby arrives with a heart open and full of love – with a great capacity to give and receive love. This is who we are. Then lots of things happen that make our hearts close – maybe a lot, maybe a little.[75] And then we think that's how we are, that's how life is.

The pristine nature with which we come into the world is never lost. This is called brilliant sanity in some Buddhist traditions. In Christian understanding, it is said that we are made like God – in God's image. You may have a phrase of your own for this understanding.

As I've said, the model one uses makes all the difference. If people come to consult with me and I see them as mainly sick and lacking, this is what I will find. If I see them as basically wise beings seeking health and life as best they can, this brings a very different quality to our meeting. A confidence in brilliant sanity is held even in the midst of what may seem like impossible conditions. It is always present.

This orientation has wide implications. It certainly means I am not grasping about for labels I can impose on the person in front of me, although the person her/himself may attach to themselves (or others) labels they've gleaned from psychology and popular reading. These terms – co-dependent, narcissistic and so on – are short cuts. But often short cuts going nowhere. They misrepresent who we are.

Brilliant sanity also means acknowledging the wisdom of the strategies the person has developed to survive and manage their lives. In Core Process the strategies that can so easily be denigrated and rather derogatively called defences are rather treated with respect and interest. We can begin to sense the effect of the defensive strategy in the body. We can appreciate it. We can let it be as it is without trying to change it. Bringing awareness is the big thing.

Core process has been described as offering a contemplative approach to relationship, to both oneself and others. So holding oneself as the practitioner with care is as important as holding the client. This is another of the important features of Core Process.

The word Core makes reference to the inherent health that is never lost, even in the midst of great difficulty. Process refers more to the patterning that may be present in our lives due to the situations and relationships we have met in the past. The two are held together in Core Process. Jung spoke similarly of the practitioner holding equally the conditioned and the universal.

Having another hold your brilliant sanity is a great gift. In Core Process the practitioner aligns themselves with this state of freedom and peace, recognising it in themselves and their clients.[76]

I'll give an illustration here to show how different it can be when brilliant sanity is not held.

I was completing the foundation course for the Karuna training in Cape Town. We were required to be in individual therapy for the four-month duration of the programme. I had not seen a therapist in this way before so I asked around and began seeing Helen, who came with high recommendations. However, she had not been trained to hold my brilliant sanity. I used to leave sessions feeling rather like the walking wounded. I remember her saying something like: 'well, we'd better not go into that as it may open up too much and you wouldn't manage since we're only meeting for four months'. I found this rather startling.

At some point I told her this story:

> I used to catch the train to and from school. I was in junior school, maybe aged about eight. I could have been older. A group of us were dashing round the coach being quite rowdy. A woman in the train said she'd be reporting us to our principal. This frightened me. The following day (which was a school day) I told my mom I had a sore foot. She was a nurse by training. She bandaged my foot, packed a picnic basket, gathered a blanket and we went and sat on the grass in the shade of the Pride of India tree in the middle of the lawn.

I'm not sure why I was telling Helen this story. Maybe I thought it was the sort of thing you did in therapy.

Helen responded, with a rather pained look on her face:

> So you couldn't tell your mother the truth.

Heck. I felt that I'd been found out. I remember leaving the session thinking how sharp she was. But I didn't feel good.

In Core Process the response might go like this:

> Oh, you sat under the tree with your mother? Can you remember the pattern on the rug? Or the quality of the light?

One would hang out with the experience, savouring it.

It's my only memory of being alone with my mother and having her kind attention to myself. (I had three siblings.)

Reflection:

Does the phrase brilliant sanity have any resonance for you? Does it seem to you a useful lens
through which to view the human condition?

The subtle field

The subtle field. This is the territory that interests the Core Process Psychotherapist. And by its very nature it is the material that, if one is not encouraged to attend to it, can be easily overlooked by practitioners and clients alike. It's like the soft voice in a conversation that you almost ignore but when you stop to wonder about what is being said, it opens whole new areas to you. I often refer to it as paying attention to the vague.

Core Process is referred to as a joint practice. So the practitioner and the client establish a field together. There is a knowing that arises here. You don't go to your head. You pay attention and knowing arises. It's a wonderful thing.

It means entering each session from a space of openness, of emptiness. The writer and psycho-analyst Wilfred Bion speaks of the practitioner being 'without memory or desire'. One has no agenda – not even that of wanting to help. This really frees things up for the practitioner and so for the client.

In more traditional psychology founded by Sigmund Freud, who I gather was a kind man (and that's so important) the territory of what became called transference and counter-transference provided information and potency in the sessions. This refers to something arising in the therapeutic space which does not necessarily 'make sense' on a cognitive level but has a certain tone to it that can hold a lot of information. Usually, however, this material is then approached in a cognitive way, with attempts to understand and interpret it. This approach doesn't adequately respect the mystery of this territory. If there is something subtly emergent in the space, to try to 'pin it down', name it, fix it to the board as one would a dead butterfly, can kill it.

Another approach would be to have a sense of wonder and enquiry regarding what has arisen. Phrases such as 'what is this?' and 'shall we stay with this a bit?' can be useful here. In Core Process, as in the tradition of Buddhism – as indeed in contemplative Christianity – awareness itself is seen as being enough. Awareness. Not interpretation, not clever ideas – though insights may arise. It is important not to apply too much effort. Maura would often remind us: no more than 25 percent effort. Effort works against the whole process. She

Presence in Relationship

speaks of finding a place between control and collapse.[77]

It's like listening to the whisper. The loud noises, the things we know, clamour for our attention. Catching the whisper. Do I hear something? What is it? Am I imagining it?

Let me give an example here.

It's the last of six sessions in the training programme I offer. I feel a sensitivity in my body – around my navel – before the session begins and this continues as we sit quietly together at the start of the morning. (This sitting quietly together feels very important, even if it's just for a few moments. It is honouring the fact that there is a wider intelligence in which we rest.) We do our usual go-round with each of us saying briefly how we find ourselves this morning or how we have been since we last met. I have a sense that something hasn't come into the room yet. Something in me just can't settle. Of course I can't really know whether this is true or just my imagination. I set the group an exercise to do individually but they ask to rather stay in the full group – which is just four people.

One of the group then says: 'Well it's all very well to learn to live more in one's body, but now I'm much more aware of my tiredness.' (Angela is the mother of three young children.) I get up to close the glass sliding door behind her. It's been bothering me that it's open. I must be feeling the need for more containment.

'Is it just this week?' I ask, as I return to my place.

'Yes,' she responds. Then she adds: 'A child died on Thursday... We knew he was going to die, but still it's been a huge shock.'

Ah, so it was this. In her saying this, the sense was of the group settling – I experienced this as myself settling. We then spent some time on the little boy who'd died, and others in the room spoke of their experience of the death of children.

This is an example of attention to the subtle. In this instance, I experienced a slight sense of disease, of not being quite settled. One notices this as it were out of the corner of one's eye, and it very often becomes clearer and finds its way to resolution – as in the above example. It all happens just through awareness.

Presence in Relationship

Sometimes people in my training groups say, 'I can't get a handle on this.' 'That's right,' I say. 'You shouldn't. That's the quality of it. It's the subtle field. It won't be grasped. That's it. Don't worry.'

Reflection:

Do you have some sense of what is meant by the subtle field? Can you remember times in your life when you've touched into this type of knowing? Is it something you feel drawn to give more attention to? How might you do this?

Embodied presence in relationship

'Embodied presence in relationship' – this is a mouth-ful. Early in our training I would some-times see this phrase and as it were, screw up my forehead. What on earth did it mean?

It means a lot to me now and almost became the title of this book – well, part of it did anyway.

We have spoken of the *brahmaviharas*. Core Process is referred to as a psychospiritual modal-ity. The resting in a wider intelligence – however one frames or images this – is essential to the work. So too is the practice of resourcing. If one shows up in the therapy room exhausted, or ar-ranges a schedule where one sees client after cli-ent with hardly a break in between, this will not produce conditions favourable to bringing pres-ence into relationship with your client.

For me, the word presence can have a big or a small 'p'. Being present in the relationship with the client is vital. And in a real sense, one is resting in a wider Presence.

I wrote in my journal recently – and the sentence moved and surprised me:

> I want someone to sit with me as if I was dying.[78]

We offer another presence at times such as birth and death. We can offer exquisite attention. Sometimes we neglect this in the time in between.

Sati – presence – is the quality that arises when we have no agenda. No agenda other than to be there and be with what arises. The ability to rest in a field of presence is a key clinical skill.[79] Franklyn explains that:

> Presence manifests as we allow our mind to still and rest wholly in present time. Our field of awareness must be whole so that we appreciate both the health and the conditions and suffering present.[80]

What does it mean to be present with the client? Well, it will generally mean more than just showing up in the room, though at times this may be all we can manage. The territory of resourcing – attending to one's own wellbeing as well as having a sense of what is happening with oneself, on an inner and outer level – creates a climate conducive to being present.

Our clients are important to us. Sometimes one is given the idea, as therapists, that your clients shouldn't matter to you. They do. Very much. But the relationship is very boundaried – and this is when it can be most effective. So it ends on time, even if the client tries to wriggle a lot against this. It is about the client's needs, not the therapist's. Sure, it's a business, but not one where one wants the client to stay at all costs. I said to my supervisor recently: 'I'd rather Richard didn't come any more and was well.' (I was referring here to a client who had suddenly stopped therapy.)

I have said that being present in the relationship with the client – or anyone for that matter – involves not having an agenda, not even an agenda for healing. There is a trust that the material the client needs to bring will naturally arise. It is simply being there, open to whatever the client brings or whatever arises in the space. This brings a beautiful sense of ease somehow. The client may have been with some very powerful material in the session the previous week and one might expect that one would continue from where he left off, but this often isn't the case at all. The person may be in quite different territory now and would be frustrated if you tried to take them back to the previous session. (This is not to say you may not refer back to what may have been very significant material at some point in subsequent sessions.)

Think of the analogy of parenting a little one. It's that moment to moment being with, knowing that they've moved on, being with them in the next moment, and not knowing where they are going to go from there. Yes, it's being out of one's depth and in a way that's far more invigorating than being *in* one's depth.[81]

And the presence one is bringing to the encounter is embodied. One is not there as a head – a cognitive, clever presence. This may be impressive for the client but it certainly doesn't heal. As Franklyn wisely says: 'Things self-organise in the presence of presence!'[82] This is my experience.

So you are with the person from moment to moment to moment to moment. We know how lovely it is when someone is willing to be with us – just that. No trying to fix, to help us even. Their presence is enough. For the practitioner, it's the willingness not to go to our head and try to figure things out. To stay present and not split off into cerebral analysis. It can be hard – and so liberating.

On the subject of presence, I was amused – and helped – by looking at notes I took of a talk back in 2002[83] where Stephen Batchelor spoke of 'waking up to our un-present'. That felt useful and not too intimidating. Noticing one's un-present. Maybe that's something we can work with.

We come from a culture which separates not only mind from body but self from other. Core Process offers remedies for this. Being present – in present time and present in one's body/mind as well as resting in Presence are key ingredients here. Remember the definition I gave of Core Process: an exploration of how we are in our present experience. The present holds all that has gone before. It is a great gift to another – as indeed to oneself – to attend to another in this way. Not trying to be smart. Just being present. It takes a lot of restraint but can be learnt.

Presence in Relationship

Reflection:

Have you had the experience of someone being present with you in this way? Or perhaps you have been with someone else? If so, how was this for you?

Is there anything about the phrase 'embodied presence in relationship' that draws you – even if you don't understand it?

Working with the body

Working with the body will, for many readers, be an unusual emphasis and I hope this introduction will at least pique your interest. It is regarded as a key area in Core Process without which healing can't really happen. Cognitive understanding on its own doesn't shift things. We all know how to be in our heads. There is no skill in that. It's the rational area that we've invested in. We value people we regard as brainy and wish we were brainy too. Cleverness is seductive. Well, this needs to change or at least be complemented by including the body.

There are an increasing number of modalities that work with the body and I think this is going to be the way of the future. It's been excluded in the West for too long. In Core Process it is one of the central aspects of the practice but it can't be isolated from resting in the *brahmaviharas* and resourcing. It is part of a full and rich enquiry with the person in front of you. Indeed for some clients, it may be a movement *away* from the body that is helpful. (Although this is far less usual.) I think of one client – she attended only one session

– who was a senior mental health worker and was additionally trained in a body modality. And yet it was difficult to get a sense of her in the room. She seemed only able to speak from her body and there wasn't, at any rate in that session, a sense of the *whole* of her.

The client is viewed as a whole – body, heart, soul, mind – all of it. By emphasising the body here one is shifting an imbalance that needs correction. So one would notice the style of the client: do they attend to details in their dress or are they relaxed about this? How do they relate to their bodies? Do they do exercise or engage in other physical practice? Do they punish their bodies through quite aggressive disciplines? One doesn't necessarily ask about this but takes it in more or less subliminally. Some clients choose to sit on the floor and others on chairs. Sitting on the floor with a supportive back rest can allow more for a sense of movement and awareness in one's torso as one is not slightly crunched up as one can be in a chair.

The practitioner notices movement in the client's body. There may be a hand gesture the client makes that they are hardly aware of. They may become somewhat breathless in parts of the session. There may be a particular way of stretching or moving, even in the chair, that is quite distinctive for a particular client. The client may be drawn to the window and to the sound of birds in the area. There may be a particular movement such as passing a hand over one's chin – a gesture I remember well from one of my clients in England.

What happens when the client is invited to notice how their body is as they relate something to you, or after they have related a particular story?

'How is your body now after telling me that?' I might ask. One doesn't make a big deal of their response. But there may be information in it.

Details can be helpful. For example:

Susan: Frances, how is your body now as you tell me you feel afraid?

Frances: It's the same. A sort of tension all over.

Susan: All through your torso?

Frances: [Nods.]

Susan: Is it anywhere in particular?

Frances: It's always here. [Indicating a sort of mid-line through her torso.]

Susan: Is it a tightness?

Frances: Yes, it's as if I'm being squeezed.

You will see in this example that Frances is not really welcoming giving me much detail but I have worked with her for several years and it does feel important to begin to understand her body sensations a little more as I sense this will be a way of knowing her more fully. I sense she is quite aware of them but seems reluctant to share these with me.

Another key aspect of the work is for the practitioner to be aware of what is happening in her own body. So whether or not the client is aware of her/his body, the practitioner is using her whole being and body as a tool in being with the client.

Sometimes even before a session, there's some subtle sensing in my body. It's not usually something that I can find a name for, but I use it as a possible clue to the session having a certain potency. Very often this does correlate with a particular space the client is in, though this may not always be the case.

As I begin to sit with the client, I may become aware that I am unable to really settle. I notice this. I have mentioned that Core Process is spoken of as a joint process. We are creating one field together and the information is present in the field. This is also the importance of the practitioner keeping current with her own process. In this way, the field can be kept relatively clear for the client's work. Of course, the therapist will have her own 'stuff' which impacts on her life, but she needs to be aware of this and be attending to it.

So I may have this sense of not quite settling and, as I have mentioned earlier, this may happen in individual work or in a group. But mostly here I am referring to individual work. This 'not-settled-ness' may give me a clue as to how the client is. I may just want to hold this in awareness. I may notice that it changes. Or I may say to the client at some point: 'Do you feel there's anything else that wants to come into the session today that hasn't quite arrived yet?'

Being with one's body at a subtle level is something that is not far from us. In his visits to people in Africa and New Mexico, Jung found people far more in touch with their bodies than Westerners typically are today.[84] In these cultures if one sensed a sort of bodily misgiving, one might well cancel one's plans and not venture out that day.

> When a Pueblo Indian does not feel in the right mood, he stays away from the men's council. When an ancient Roman stumbled on the threshold as he left his house, he gave up his plans for the day.[85]

In bringing one's somatic[86] attention into the space with one's client, one might notice different things. So one's eyes may become a bit blurry. This one gets to recognise as a possible sense of shock in the room. (I will say more on this in the section on shock and trauma.) This blurriness or slight wooziness is important and must be respected. It will generally indicate that the client is in delicate territory and the non-verbal space will need to be attended to as this is usually beyond the realm of the cognitive and language alone. It can be experienced as an uncomfortable feeling.

Similarly, if a client reports a sensation in one or both of their eyes this can be a sign of some delicate process wanting attention. The eyes can indicate a lot in the territory of shock and trauma.

To return to the body of the practitioner. If I settle easily into the space, I can fairly firmly assume that the client is doing the same. Glenda came to see me for several months. By her second session, she seemed so firmly 'settled in' that it struck me as odd. (I experienced this as a sense of settled-ness in my own body.) It was so striking that I felt I needed to mention it.

Susan: You seem to have settled here so quickly.

Glenda: Yes, I do that. We moved 18 times when I was a child and I was always going to new schools. I know how to settle really quickly.

I was so glad we had 'clocked' that together. It felt rather sad.

And yet Glenda 'unsettled' quickly too and in an e-mail told me, after about six months, that she would be moving on to start work with another therapist.

People have different patterns of ending and it is the unusual client – in my experience – who can really work with ending and do that in relationship to and with the therapist. As I say in my contract, it is useful if the work around ending can be done together.

Reflection:

Does this territory of the body interest you? Do you find yourself sceptical about it? If you left that scepticism aside, what else would there be?

Working from the body

As I have said, including the body in the work is an unusual emphasis for many people. Let me say very directly that I had no clue what people were on about in my training – probably for the first few years – when there was an encouragement to be with the body. I didn't understand what they were talking about. So take heart!

In the *Rohitassa Sutta*, the Buddha says of the body:

> Within this fathom long body... there is the cosmos, the origination of the cosmos, the cessation of the cosmos.[87]

In some ways the whole of our work in Core Process Psychotherapy is to be simply present and fully embodied.[88]

Others like Leonardo da Vinci have, either in words or images, shown the majesty of the body and how it is connected to a far wider field than we easily understand.

For some of us, being in the body has been a difficult place to be. While the territory of thoughts and feelings may be well known to many of us, the body is often less so. Giving attention to the body has an immediacy and can make the work fresh and interesting. As Margaret Wilkinson, the Jungian psychoanalyst and writer, says: 'Thinking is doing it the hard way' – speaking of our innate capacity for empathy that includes the body.[89] The split between the mind and the body requires healing and it is crucial – when with a client – to engage at levels not including speech. The attunement and listening is with the whole body. The journey back to the body, though, can be a long one.

I will say more here of my experience of using my body directly in work with my clients. This is not something I particularly speak to them about as I think that could feel intrusive. After I have worked with someone for a period of time, and if the field is fairly settled, at times I disclose a body sensation I am aware of. So I may ask:

Susan: How are you doing in your body right now?

Client: [Looks blank.]

Susan: I was asking as I sense a slight sensation in my heart area.

The type of sensations I notice in myself include the following: a tenderness around my heart; a sensation behind one of my shoulders; flashes of a headache; a blurriness in my eyes; a tingling in my hands or other parts of my body; or indeed a sense of settledness, groundedness, spaciousness. Equally, I might experience an inability to settle. Typically the sensation would only last for a few seconds or maybe half a minute.

By giving light attention to my body sensations, they serve as a tool for me – a way of sensing into the space and what is going on in it. I am curious about tensions or sensations that arise in my body while with the client and these sometimes prompt me to ask the client what they are aware of in their body. In this, I am certainly not suggesting they change anything. It is just inviting them to notice their experience.

Sometimes one may sense a bit of a disconnect between what the client says and the feeling in the room. So a client may be relating an everyday event of perhaps visiting a mall and yet one has a strange sense of sadness. Or the following may happen, as was the case with a client recently:

Paula: I feel so afraid. It's just too much. Too much has been happening. When is my suffering going to end? Why am I singled out for so much pain?

I could, of course, hear what Paula was saying and what she was saying was entirely reasonable in terms of her life experience and the extremely rough cards she'd been dealt, but my body felt very settled.

It wouldn't be sensitive to say anything at the time, but before the end of the session I found myself telling Paula about this.

Susan: When the session started you weren't feeling good at all. You were very frightened. And yet I felt good in myself and settled. This suggests to me that there might also be goodness in where you are right now. You have done a huge amount of such courageous work. It may well be that you are coming to the end of a period of processing huge pain.

I like to work in a spacious room and to be able to offer the client the opportunity to stand and to move around the room, if they would like to.

Should they do this, I would stand or move with them, continuing the practice of awareness now from a different bodily posture. (It is very seldom that a client responds to this, though when I am a client I like to make use of the space.)

I may use my body in the space in a way I will illustrate now, though this is highly unusual for me.

To return to Paula. She was being impacted by very traumatic material from previous generations, having grown up in the shadow of war.

Paula: I've been dumped on. I feel like a rape victim. Why does everyone dump on me?

Susan: What is the image of this? What does this 'dumped on' feeling look like?

Paula: I'm covered in rubbish.

Susan: So it's like there's a big pile of rubbish on top of you?

Paula: Yes, that's right.

Susan: Can you be seen in this pile?

Paula: No, I'm completely covered.

Susan: Can you move out from there?

Paula: I can't. What will happen if I move away from there? Who's going to take the rubbish?

Susan: [After a little more conversation] ...Can I talk to the child in the pile? [Paula had been referring to herself as a child.]

Paula agreed and I sort of crouched next to what I imagined to be a pile of rubbish and mess to the side of me. I spoke to the little girl.

Susan: Paula, are you in there? I know you are. I'm here. You're still alive. I want you to come out of there with me.

I asked the little girl to reach out her hand, take mine and we'd walk away together, leaving behind us the mass of devastation. It was time to leave it behind.

This was highly unusual for me but for various reasons it seemed appropriate – or not inappropriate – with this particular client at this time. In the course of the following session, I asked Paula:

'How was that exercise I did about pulling you out of the pile? Was it unhelpful?' – as I had been wondering if it had been.

'No,' she said. 'All the little things you do are helpful in some way as they help me know another way is possible.'

So the practitioner's body is very much part of the session. There's a creativity and a fluidity in this, although mostly sessions look very ordinary. This ordinariness can almost be a hallmark of Core Process. And yet profound work is going on.

Desire can arise in the therapeutic space. It is important to give this attention in supervision. It can be a beautiful thing for the client that desire can come into the space and be received there. Erotic desire in therapy is at times given bad press as it's quite tricky territory, but essentially it's full of life and vitality. Here, as always, one offers spacious attention and gentle awareness. Like any other territory, this will have many textures and will shift and change from moment to moment. It does not need to be feared. (I mentioned the Buddhist teaching on impermanence at the beginning of the book. One is aware of change and movement from moment to moment in the work).

Let me touch again on the subject of emotional expression. Frequently these days, there is an encouragement to articulate one's emotional state. One might however question whether this is always useful, though for many of us it has been a struggle and it has taken courage to learn to express ourselves in this way. To a question regarding the value of emotional expression in therapy, Maura responded thus:

> Emotional expression is neither good nor bad... Most of what looks like catharsis is actually re-traumatisation... The things that usually make the expression of emotion more appropriate are presence, contact and relationship.[90]

She suggests that the expression of emotion can be judged by its consequence: was that helpful? Did it free something?[91] This is something into which we can enquire.

In bringing awareness to the body or the somatic dimension, one generally doesn't then proceed to analyse the sensation the client or the practitioner is experiencing. There is a lightness to it. One moves on. Though if the client experiences a strong sensation, I will often check in later with them as to whether or not the sensation is still present. Usually it will have changed. It is often very unremarkable. It's the client's process and they generally lead this. The usefulness in the body as 'access' to the person, if you like, is that it has a quality of presence – present-time-ness. It doesn't lie.

I find most clients are interested in including their body in the work, though this is something I introduce quite gently. And sometimes I may not introduce it at all. Thus far there's been only one client that comes to mind who would bat me off if I asked her if she noticed anything regarding her body. She explained she wasn't comfortable with the question as she generally couldn't sense anything. I appreciated her clear 'no' on this. It was in keeping with her directness as a person.

Reflection:

Is there anything that particularly interests you in this section? Do you know why this strikes you? Do you have a sense of where you might want to go with this?

The body remembers

In including the body as a key tool in the work, we are not doing this as some trendy technique. Nor do we try to figure out what it is that the body may be remembering in its various sensations and tones. We simply bring awareness to this as we do to other areas of arising in the work.

It is clear that the body does remember – the body knows.[92] It remembers at the level of body tone and sensation though perhaps not in direct expressible detail, as much of the remembering may come from a time before there was speech and words to make sense of experience.

This is not to say that the practitioner's mind may not continue working – one may get a thousand bright ideas. Practising restraint is vital. Hold back. Hold out. Hold on. Don't impose yourself on the client's process. This isn't the same as not being involved. The involvement is profound. The exercise I share in the next section will be one in which restraint is taught and, as I'll be pointing out, it can feel most frustrating!

Many of us live in a general state of alertness. Maura says that one's whole life can be mediated through fear. In this case, there is a subtle cellular protection present that cannot be worked with through the usual cognitive psychological approaches.[93] This very subtle contracting or pushing away can loosen and be transformed in the process of the work. Typically, it will happen slowly over time. I have always appreciated the words of Thanissara[94] who spoke of valuing the small shifts as these are usually more easily integrated than the larger shifts that most of us might long for.

One client experienced a sense of release at a cellular level in a period of meditation and recounted this to me:

> My cells were rejoicing. That's the only way I can put it. All the trillions of tiny tiny cells. They were happy. Like a baby who is held and well cared for.

This was her lived experience, if only for a few moments. This was an exceptional experience for a person who lived with a sense of constriction and contraction in her body from a lifetime of vigilance and guardedness.

Reflection:

I seem to have no words here for a reflection –
perhaps as we are in the territory of no words.

Does the heading 'The Body Remembers' stir anything in you?

When two or three: exchanges

I think Jesus knew what he was on about when he said: where there are two or three together, there is p/Presence.[95]

Much has been written about what size group works. I am a bit of a fan of the small group – me and three or four others is fine. In other contexts, me and another is fine – for example, when offering mutual support.

I want to offer you a form that was used extensively in my training and which I now use in the training I offer. It is called exchanges. It is a precious resource.

It is simple – as usually the best forms are – and involves two direct questions:

What's happening now?

How is that for you?

The minimum number for this work is three. This may also be the optimal number. One person takes the role of the client, one as therapist and the other as witness. If there are additional people, they can also be witnesses. In a much bigger group, some members could each hold one of the *brahmaviharas*.

For the client, it is an opportunity for an enquiry – to explore his/her own experience as he/she sits. The person may use the space to talk about something that's bothering them. They may begin with no sense of what they want to say – this is sometimes best. Or they may use the time as an opportunity to sense into their body. It offers a person a lot to have a free space where they're not going to be interrupted by smart thoughts or the curiosity of the person serving as therapist. (As yes, happens in the consulting room!)

The therapist can only use the two questions stated above: 'What's happening now?' and 'How is that for you?' One question usually follows the other. The spacing of the questions is up to the person asking them.

For some people, it can feel extremely restraining to have only these two questions. One might long to grunt, do something, anything but just sit there being with two simple questions. (It can be useful here to remember the practice of holding wide attention, and returning to resource and a sense of ground.) Equally, it can feel beautiful to work with such simplicity.

I usually start with people doing the exercise for five or seven minutes. And gradually, we build up the time over the period of a few months. In my own training in England, this was the bones, as it were, of our training. I think we increased the time until we were doing a full hour. If my memory serves me correctly, we did this throughout the intensive part of the training – three years.

The role of the witness is quite subtle. S/he should not focus intently on the client or the therapist. That would be a bit unnerving for them. It's rather that the witness stays in their own ground/resource. There is a sense of the witness' presence being supportive. But the witness is also noticing what arises for her as she sits. Does a great sleepiness come over her suddenly? Does she itch? Does she get frustrated on the therapist's behalf? The witness will be picking up on what is happening in the field. Anything can happen. Be with your own experience as you sit.[96]

After the agreed time is complete, there is a short period for feedback. The client would speak last here. So each person is invited – and this is the tricky part – *not* to analyse what they felt about what went on in the session, what could have been better, what was very good and so on (this can be extremely hard to resist at first). Rather, they are invited to share what they were aware of in themselves in the session. A sense of rest? A sense of the time being short? A sleepiness? Nothing is silly here. So if the exchange was seven minutes, the feedback would be about five minutes in total. Don't drag it out. Each person needs to have a turn. Then the group would change round, taking care that the person who had played the role of client is now in the role of witness so that h/she has a chance to settle with the experience s/he has just had. Of course, each person's experience is quite different. For some, it may feel quite mundane. Others may be profoundly struck by something that arises.

I think the exercise is called exchanges as one does get a sense of sitting in one field and that subtle material arises and may be subliminally shared between the participants.

The two questions have an obvious immediacy

to them. They are designed to enable the person receiving them to be with their direct experience – whether this is of stillness, having a head full of thoughts or a silliness. And the follow-up question is an enquiry into the client's relationship to this territory. The aim is not to alter the experience but to sense how the person relates to it.[97] So it could run something like this:

Therapist: What's happening now?

Client: [Long pause] ...Nothing really.

Therapist: How is that for you?

Client: It's quite peaceful actually. Hmmm.

Therapist: [After a pause] ...What's happening now?

Client: Still peaceful.

It may be as unspectacular as that. And as restful. We don't need to always chase the exciting storyline.

Reflection:

Do you have some sense of the exchanges process? Does it feel like something you'd like to try? If so, can you set up the conditions for this – for example, ask a friend to do it with you? If there is not a witness you can go ahead anyway. Do it with intention and care. Spend a little time calling to mind the *brahmaviharas* before you begin or have a short time of silence. You may like to do the grounding exercise. Remain faithful to the questions. Remember in the feedback not to go into analysing mode.

PART
3

In this section, I will be reflecting on matters of individual, societal and global significance. I will name different territories but do not look at any of them in great detail.

Suffering in our global world

I begin with suffering in our global world.

Growing up and living most of my adult life in South Africa – and for part of that time living and working in very impoverished rural areas of our country – I easily associated suffering with physical deprivation, hunger, lack of services and so on. When we think of suffering in the global world, this is where our attention easily goes. However I now view the situation in a more nuanced way.

Those of us in the West[98] can be rather patronising towards people in the developing world and would perhaps like to put a distance between ourselves and those in the two-thirds world (as it has been helpfully called) by regarding the situation of these people as rather pathetic. I sometimes hear women in what I am calling the West, sympathise superficially with the plight of women in the two-thirds world and yet they themselves seem to ignore the oppression in their own lives – for example, by staying in an unloving relationship because of its promise of financial security.

Liberation theology emerged in the church in around the 1980s in South America. There was the assertion that Jesus was on the side of the poor – he has a preferential option for the poor is how it was often put. This was an exciting movement which encouraged people to think for themselves, analyse their situation and act for justice. It built solidarity and was feared by those in power. It was useful and indeed liberating. (Having spent some time in a seminary at around the time of transition in South Africa I had a real sense of the energy of this movement and I loved it.)

But this is not the whole story. And different times demand different responses. I would argue that the need today is at least equally among the so-called rich. Their suffering too deserves attention.

As I have indicated, I spent about 10 years of my professional life working in marginalised communities with people in extreme poverty. By this I mean that people were hungry and had very limited diets – though they prepared simple and delicious meals from their very basic provisions – had inadequate health care, and young people would often drop out of school due to a lack of funds. I must add that this was one of the richest periods of my life.

Working with such communities, in some ways, distanced me from my own pain and the wound-edness of my own culture. It was only when I did the psychotherapy training course in England that I began to acknowledge my own wounding and that of my culture. (I am a South African of English descent so my ancestors were impacted by both wars in Europe in the 20th century.) This I regard as a very important development for me and made me a far more integrated person.

While justice remains a huge concern and the dis-parity in the world is completely untenable for ev-eryone, I am now also aware and concerned with the suffering of those who are materially well off. Studies suggest that mental anguish in these com-munities is more acute and endemic. The winners are really the losers I fear.[99] People in the West are dying from isolation. We speak of the need for community development invariably in connec-tion with poor communities, but it is also richer communities that could benefit hugely from this. Notes I have on development philosophy say that development should lead to the de-alienation of the individual.[100] How we need this in the West.

Of course, this isn't a matter of either/or. All communities require this in different ways. The difference is that richer communities seldom acknowledge their need. Perhaps we need a handbook on this. There have been many manuals written for community development among the poor, but few for the rich. At this stage of my life, I am working largely among the 'haves'. As I have stated in an earlier publication, *Pleasure-in-relating:* 'everybody's suffering is valid'.[101]

Reflection:

How do you respond to the point I'm making that suffering is not just a problem in poorer communities? Do you think it may be true that in wealthier communities too there is huge suffering? What is your experience of this?

The dynamic cycle

Frank Lake, a Christian psychiatrist, used the term 'the dynamic cycle'.[102] I'll explain briefly what he meant by this.

Generally, it is taught that the early years of the child are of great importance developmentally. And so they are. But what Lake is saying is that development is dynamic. So whatever one's age, one can re-visit earlier developmental stages and healing can happen.

The term 'neural plasticity' is becoming quite popular. This refers to the ability of our nervous system to change, to mend itself, whatever age we are. So while in children we see changes happening almost day by day, as adults and older people we too are capable of movement and change. What good news!

Reflection:

Whatever your age at present, do you recognise your capacity for change? Does this possibility excite you? Do you have a sense of what might support this?

Depression

Enquiry into depression is important as it is so pervasive and I keep feeling we misunderstand it. Thinking we understand something tends to be dangerous. I remember Daniel, a client in England. He was about 60 then. He was an interesting and talented man with many skills. And yet he just couldn't really crack anything in his life. There was a sense of misery about him. It felt we easily got stuck in the mire in our sessions. (And sure, sometimes staying in stuckness with someone is all we can do.)

As I think of him, I wonder if we get into a sort of groove of depression. You could almost envisage it as a deep rut. Once you're in it you can't see beyond the sides of it. It can feel like all there is, when in fact it may only be part of the landscape. We often know the groove really well. The challenge may sometimes be to notice that there is a landscape beyond this. A friend has said this is part of the tough-ness of depression for her – its all-pervasiveness.

I am seeking to understand. There's too much

suffering out there.

I wonder what would have happened if Daniel and I had deliberately side-stepped the depression groove in our sessions. Would this have been possible? I remember so clearly doing this myself once while out walking through what is called a green belt here – a shady walk along a river. I was overcome by a sticky 'ugh-y' mood – I don't really know what to call it. It was pretty intolerable. I experimented with imagining (I don't think I actually did it, but I may have) stepping to the side of this. So literally stepping out of that space. To my huge surprise, it worked. I could step out of it. That's not to say it may not slither back, but the sense that I could choose to almost move around it was very liberating. This is a fine line as emotional tones that arise may be asking for attention and hold some information for us.

I asked to speak to my friend Anita about depression and medication. Of her own experience, she says:

> When I was in my 20s I went on anti-depressants for the first time. I needed to. They saved my life. Then in my 40s I went on them for the second

time. This I feel was a mistake. I think I
needed to be depressed.

I found this helpful. It seems that if you are found
to be depressed, rather than looking at what the
contributing factors are to this, the first line of
treatment is often to go onto medication. Sure,
one may then manage one's life situation better,
but it may mean not making the changes your
psyche is calling for you to make. This may become
evident should you stop taking the medication and
have not made the necessary adjustments in your
inner or outer world. You may well then decide
you need to return to the medication as you feel
no better. But that may surely be, at least in part,
because you have not addressed your situation.

Anita also mentioned that when she was on anti-
depressants, she felt there was a sort of a screen
between herself and the rest of the world. She
says she senses that now, at times, with people
who are on medication.

I'm not saying don't go on anti-depressants. But
know why you're going on them. Have a plan. I
think exploring this gently with a therapist is
good. There may certainly be times when I would
support a person getting medical support in this

way – though I may also help them look into natural alternatives. But a gung ho approach – just go on meds! – is unimaginative and doesn't really serve us or our planet. It is the rare medical practitioner who will concede that the whole medication thing is very experimental and we don't really know what we're doing (this with regard to mental health). Studies support this with people on medication not doing much better, if at all, than those taking placebo or no treatment.

Perhaps it's our intolerance of suffering that is the problem. Perhaps our suffering wants to be known. And our inner resources strengthened. In *Pleasure-in-relating,* I quote from an article by Mark Rice-Oxley, writing of his own experience of depression where he says four things helped him: 'Meditation, love, time and therapy.'[103] That would seem to be a good treatment plan. There is so much more on offer than medication.

Reflection:

Have you suffered from what you would call depression? If so, how did you deal with this and what did you learn from the experience?

Do you think I'm being naïve or even uncaring here? Where do you differ with me?

Psychosis

Psychosis is another area of mystery. If we remember that psyche means soul, psychosis is then perhaps a sickness of the soul. The soul is needing attention, care.

An acquaintance spent a good part of a year attending to her son who was in his 30s and had become psychotic. I was interested in what she told me of the experience some years later.

She said that Peter had several different episodes of being, as they say, out of contact with reality. And yet she said if you listened carefully, there was sense in what he was saying. One of the episodes appeared to deal with the abuse his mother (my friend) had suffered at the hands of her stepfather many years before when she was a young girl. (The son had been aware of this as he had been told about it by his mother.) Another psychotic episode dealt with another ancestral matter – I don't remember the details now. There was a sense of progression in the material Peter was dealing with. Was he undergoing a form of healing that was going back down the generations?

The experience was exhausting and painful – for Peter and his loving family and friends. But there seemed to be sense in it. (And he's much better now.)

Each of our psyches has this capacity to sort of shut off or go into a different mode when things get too much. We may require care rather than hospitalisation at such a time.

One of our senior tutors spoke of how she'd travelled to America from England to follow a psychiatrist boyfriend at a time in her youth. The relationship hadn't worked out and she arrived back in Heathrow, London, and completely lost the plot. She had to receive loving care from friends for several months before she recovered.

A person in a psychotic state can be 'met'. A South African psychiatrist John Parker has said:

> I can engage with someone who's completely psychotic. It's about learning to speak to the human deep inside there.[104]

I have recently become aware of compelling work being done in Finland.[105] A unit there has by far the best results for treating psychosis in the western world. (And interestingly, the results in India and Nigeria are far better than those in the West.) Why is this? There is minimum interference of a medical nature. In Finland medication is very rarely prescribed. Every attempt is made not to hospitalise people but rather to treat them in their homes. People are spoken to in ordinary language. In Finland several staff members meet with the patient and their family. There is open discussion as to the best way of assisting the person. The patient/client themselves would be very much part of this. The professionals might disagree with each other and they'd be open about this in the gathering. It's all normalised. And the results speak for themselves.

I'm suggesting that psychotic experiences are part of the psyche's range of experience. The challenge is not to be too afraid of the distressing symptoms that appear. And clearly a team approach is needed to support the person. There is so much we don't know. But let's try to trust the natural processes of our psyches. And I must add that being the therapist of someone who is going through such a process is worrying. I am certainly not suggesting that the situation is not distressing and challenging. But it can be met.

Reflection:

Do you remember having any experience that may have been psychotic or close to it? Have you been involved with others – even indirectly – who have had this experience? What are your insights in this regard?

The perinatal field

In the second year of our training, we begin to explore the perinatal field. It is fascinating territory. This is the early period from conception through birth to the first nine months of life. (Perinatal literally means around the time of birth.) We know now that this period is key for the child's – and the person's – later development. We refer to the themes and patterns that are laid down during this period as primary patterning – the earliest form of patterning.

Laura Donington articulates this helpfully in her article on Core Process Psychotherapy:

> The primary experiences around conception... gestation and birth give rise to some of the deepest conditioning which patterns much of how we meet subsequent experience in the world... This primary patterning provides the matrix for later experience.[106]

In Core Process the therapist is trained to include this area of the client's life in the enquiry you're engaged in together. It is interesting how often material from this territory arises in the consulting room. As in this stage of life there are no words, the territory is of a non-verbal nature. I will give some examples of how this might arise using examples from clients and from my own direct experience.

I think of Rashied. He is a relatively young man and a highly trained professional who has had several extremely demanding jobs. He would sometimes describe getting into a place which he called 'the zone'. It would be as if he was in a tunnel or some sort of big bubble. In this space, he felt pretty invincible. This was a space in which he could live for weeks at a time if, for example, he had a complicated project to complete. He would hardly sleep during this time.

This was a space Rashied knew well and which he valued. However, we were also beginning to recognise that after months in 'the zone', his physical and mental health would deteriorate. So while appreciating this space as having been useful in enabling him to achieve certain results and to survive some demanding situations, Rashied began to realise it was preferable that he had more choice about whether to go into the zone and perhaps slowly create a life where the zone was no longer necessary.

Rashied had spent the first part of his life in an incubator, having been born with jaundice. Sometimes in sessions, it would be as if we were entering a sort of twilight zone. A kind of wooziness would enter the space.

Susan: What's happening now?

Rashied: I'm not quite sure. There's something strange going on.

Susan: Yes, I have a sense of a sort of blurriness in the space. Is this your experience?

Rashied: Yes.

Susan: It makes me wonder about the time you spent in the incubator as a baby.

Rashied: Yes, I think that might be it. How strange...

The relationship between the incubator-type space and the zone wasn't exactly clear to us, but precise details do not matter here. One brings awareness to what arises and feels into the texture of the space. It is rather difficult to describe in words as this is from a pre-verbal period in Rashied's life so there is necessarily a great subtlety to the experience.

It's useful to bear the territory of the perinatal in mind as sometimes there's nothing else that might explain a particular space or tone in the room, but when the client's early history is acknowledged there can be a sense of a 'fit'.

Another client Belinda was born with a physical abnormality and needed to have surgery in the first few weeks of her life and at intervals after that. In our work together, a certain atmosphere would enter the room. At times this was accompanied by Belinda looking pale and not well at all. These times of hospitalisation had been very hard in that they involved separation from her mother.

These early stages of life need at least equal attention to other parts of the client's life that may be expressed more easily as they were experienced in a time of language. I find that clients often recognise the importance of this territory and do not regard it as bizarre that this early time should be impacting on their present life many years later.

I have described Core Process Psychotherapy as an exploration of how we are in our present experience and how this expresses the past conditioning and conditions of our lives. Perhaps this definition now makes more sense. Our earliest experience can colour how we experience the present.

Again there is nothing to be 'done' with this space apart from bringing awareness to it.

In our training, we are also taught to be with movements that might want to happen in the body. I remember myself as a client sitting in therapy and it was as if a movement forward wanted to happen – as if I wanted to fall forward. My therapist found a way of supporting me doing this. (I think she placed some cushions in front of me so that I would land softly.) It seemed clear to both of us that this was something to do with my birth process. In a situation like this, one might actually complete the movement or imagine oneself doing this.

It is concerning that so many women now are choosing to have caesarean sections. I say this as there is, of course, a natural beauty and design to our birth process. The pushing of the baby is important. I remember one member of our training group who had been born by caesarean section. When we were doing practical exercises around birth, he worked with this. It was as though his birth process was still incomplete.

It seems clear that a client can't go to territory unless s/he feels the therapist will be able to hold them in this. If you work as a therapist, it is useful if you can be open to and trusting of this very early experience, and allow it to be present in your work with clients. If necessary, one should seek training to equip oneself for this aspect of the work.

The perinatal period includes the time in the womb. There is a cellular learning in the womb that can flavour adult life. The developing foetus is influenced by the mother's feelings and her situation during pregnancy. Franklyn uses the phrase 'womb as world' to indicate how your experience in the womb can colour your life experience as an adult.

Let me add here that there is also a sense that the being entering the world comes with its own disposition and character. So although the conditions s/he meets from conception on are influential, there is also the individuality of the being him/

herself being incarnated into our world. It can be useful to remember this.

Reflection:

What is your response to this material? Are you intrigued by it? For further reading you could start with *Why Love Matters: How affection shapes a baby's brain* by Sue Gerhardt. It's a lovely book.

Attachment

There is a lot written in psychology on what is called attachment theory. Attachment theory regards the ability of the child to attach to another human being as a key indicator of health in the individual. It enquires into the early child-rearing experienced by the person and how this might have impacted on the way the individual now meets others in their world. Attachment is based on the human need for security and love.

Many of us are wounded at this level of attachment.

People in my generation and with my background grew up in the wake of horrendous wars in Europe in which many of our parents lost their fathers – either literally or they were lost to us in other ways in that they could not be available to us because of their own damage. This was the case too with some of our mothers.

Whatever the case, many of us did not receive the sensitive care we needed in our early lives. While we may have been breastfed, the feeding may not have been responsive to us – in terms of its timing and the kindness with which it was done.

As a consequence, many of us have challenges at the level of intimacy. A lot of us will experience profound and confusing ambivalence when it comes to relational intimacy – and I am not only referring to sexual intimacy here, though this is included.

Where the caregiver is severely depressed, this is very difficult for the little being. The child may then start taking care of the mother and in intimate relationships in later life, may need to be overly caring to their partner to the point of suffocation. The child builds up a model of its relational world based on the nature of its interactions with primary caregivers. This leads to her/his basic assumptions about the world. Part of the work of therapy is to hold these frames in the light of awareness.[107]

Attachment theorists describe several attachment patterns that result from different patterns of parenting.

One of the patterns we dealt with in my training – and the one that involves the most profound degree of suffering – is called transmarginal stress.[108] This is the situation where the infant has not been responded to adequately and so as an adult, longs for but also deeply fears intimacy. Transmarginal stress – stress beyond the margins of what is tolerable – is the name for this affliction. Maura and Franklyn explain this by saying that for such people, the pain of the possibility of being loved can be harder than that of not being loved. The very thing that is desired – contact and intimacy – is experienced as threatening. The person is placed in a double bind. Due to one's early experience, intimacy is experienced as overwhelming.

I remember a lecture where the speaker, a psychotherapist, related the fact that he could not remain in an intimate relationship until he met the woman he would later marry. I remember him saying that she just didn't go away. She could tolerate the nightmarish spaces he went into. Many couples would not survive this.

Maura speaks of the healing that can come from relationship – including the psychotherapeutic relationship – as one is welcomed back into the warmth of human contact. She encouragingly says that defences against being loved erode over time.[109] Trust in intimacy can be slowly renegotiated.[110] Let us take comfort from this. In psychotherapeutic work, one aspect of attachment theory that is very important is that of the secure base or safe holding environment. It is this still and reliable field that is essential in enabling the client to bring what s/he needs into the space. In the consistent steadiness and compassion that can be offered in the therapeutic relationship, there is another chance to find someone who can respond to one appropriately and adequately. As Maxine Linnell said in our foundation training: Wounding happens in relationship, so healing too will happen in relationship.[111]

Reflection:

Do you have any sense of your pattern of attachment? How do you know this? Do you have a sense of what you might need in this regard?

Attachment: holding a sense of the other

Writing in the 1950s, psychoanalyst and paediatrician Donald Winnicott coined the term the 'good-enough parent'. This phrase has given comfort to many. Good-enough parenting can result in the person being able to hold a sense of the presence of the caregiver even if that person is not with them – either due to absence or death.

Some people are not able to access this 'internal other' and rest in the holding that might come from this.

I read a most moving story lately entitled *The Man of Good Hope*. The author Jonny Steinberg relates the true story of a man from Somalia, Asad Abdullahi, who travelled through the African continent to Cape Town. At home in Somalia, aged eight, the little boy is with his mother and the other children when attackers come to the door. His mother tries to keep the door closed but they burst through and she is shot dead as Asad clings to her legs. And yet as this adult man later travels through his continent and faces extreme challenges, he carries the presence of his mother with him and is very clear that he does that. She has never left him. This indigenous African example has a huge amount to teach us.

In the story, Asad has just given Jonny an account of his mother's death. A few days after her death, he and his siblings leave Mogadishu. Steinberg writes:

> As I picture Asad heading farther from home I think more than anything else, not of what he left behind but of what he took with him. He would never again be firmly moored to any particular adult, to any family. He would become a child whose connections to others would dissolve and re-form and disappear again. And yet he says with certainty that on his great journey through childhood and across the African continent he took his mother.
>
> He has no memory of her face, nor of the sound of her voice: her place inside him is more ambient than that, more powerful. It is indistinguishable

Presence in Relationship

from his sense of himself, of why he is a man who works hard and is kind and finds things funny; indeed, why he is the sort of man who can share such memories and keep his composure.

'If there is such a thing as a best mother, mine was it,' [Asad] says... I last saw her at such a young age. The way she taught me, although I grew up an orphan, I still feel that what she was I am today. I did not lose her despite her death. I am not sure that words can describe what I am trying to tell you. I mean that by the time I was seven, she had already made me.'[112]

Asad says poignantly: 'I remember that she enjoyed being with us.'[113] This is a key quality to offer another. And of course it can't be forced.

Later in the book Steinberg writes [and Asad is in pretty challenging circumstances at the time]:

Without warning, he [Asad] felt the presence of his mother. He thought of the two thick plaits of hair running down her back, and he realised that

the image was not really as powerful as the feeling and that the feeling was indescribable. She was with
him always; something truly terrible
would have to happen to shake her
out. He recalls the revelation coming
to him on the back of Rooda's truck,
the wind in his face, the yellow desert
all around.[114]

This 'good attachment' Asad then passes on to his
own children. Towards the end of the book, when
the family are now in America and Asad's daughter Rahma is two, Jonny writes:

She and Asad have long conversations,
he in Somali, she in her gobbledygook.
They are always eye to eye when they
talk: she stands on her father's thighs
and holds his face, feeling for the vi-
brations of his voice in his jaws. She
will not take her eyes off him, will not
stop touching him. When he is walking around the house, she is wrapped
around his back. When he is talking to
me, she is curled up in his lap. When
we eat a meal, she sits on his knee and
eats from his plate.[115]

As much as good attachment is easily passed on, so of course are less satisfactory attachment processes. And this is where Core Process and other therapeutic modalities come into their own – offering to the person what could not be offered in their infancy and childhood.

Reflection:

What strikes you about this section?

Are you moved by Asad's story? What is your own experience in this regard – do you have a sense of the presence of a dear one within you that accompanies you through life?

Sex and intimacy

Sexual intimacy, despite what the adverts, romantic novels and films may suggest, is not necessarily straightforward.

I am beginning to realise that many spiritual leaders have experienced some early breech in relationship and it is quite likely this that has led them to pursue a spiritual enquiry.

I was recently struck by reading the story of Siddhartha Gautama (the person who became known as the Buddha). It is recounted – as I understand it in all records of his early upbringing – that his mother died in childbirth. A contemporary South African writer Antony Osler, in his own account of the Buddha's life, goes on to say that Siddhartha's father rejected the child at first.[116] This would make sense in the light of the father's grief at his wife's death. According to Antony's account, the child was raised by loving people but they were not from his family. My sense is that this early shock contributed to Siddhartha as a young man embarking on a search for meaning. Osler writes (and remember, it is his own interpretation of the Buddha's life) that Siddhartha could not relate intimately to his wife or the child she bore. This is resonant with the experience of one who was not well met himself in infancy. I have written elsewhere that our gifts and our wounds are like two sides of one coin.[117] It was his suffering, as for so many of us, that led to his enquiry.

Since reading about Siddhartha, I keep being struck by spiritual leaders who have suffered grave loss in early childhood. Thomas Merton, a contemplative Christian monk, lost his mother at age six and thereafter was cruelly treated by his stepmother. (His father died when he was 16.) An account I read of the prophet Mohammad's life, states that his father died before his birth and his mother was in such difficult circumstances that she could not care for the child who then lived with a Bedouin family till the age of six. Shortly after he returned to his mother, she died. 'This double bereavement made a deep impression on Muhammad,' writes the author Karen Armstrong.[118]

Regarding sexual intimacy, one may be in an intimate relationship but have a complicated relationship with genital sex. For some, their experience of genital sex is that they sort of flip out. Something gets triggered and they go into a space of a lot of difficulty and strangeness. This is not territory that is easily understood or explained. It would be in the territory of transmarginal stress that I spoke about earlier.

I was heartened to read somewhere – I think in a book of essays of a spiritual nature – of two men who lived together in a committed and loving relationship but their relationship was not sexual in the usual sense of the word as one of the men could not tolerate this. It is good for us to know that in the event of wounding of this nature, there are ways of being in a committed and loving relationship which can accommodate our particular vulnerability – in this instance in the area of genital sexual expression. It is useful to be open to the many ways one can structure a relationship.

There are also people for whom the sexual encounter appears uncomplicated when it is more recreational but becomes fraught and overwhelming when linked to true intimacy with another. As you can imagine, this is painful and delicate territory to negotiate.

What I am suggesting in this section is that early trauma can result in certain difficulties in 'being in this world' which may also manifest in challenges regarding intimacy. These very challenges, however, can lead a person to profound areas of enquiry that are enriching for themselves and others. In the event of it contributing to a person's spiritual enquiry, through this same exploration the person may, as it were, find their way back to humanity and be able to offer this integration to the world.

Reflection:

Is there anything that particularly moves you in this section?

If you get a sense of your own wounded-ness here, perhaps don't rush on right now.

Working with diversity

It is lovely to work with difference in psycho-therapy and life in general. In many parts of the world, there is now ample opportunity for this. Difference can be delighted in.

With sexual orientation, however open one is, being different in one's sexual identity is not easy to welcome – at least initially. It can be quite difficult territory for people to raise 'wonderings' around sexual identity in a therapy session. Clients seem helped and relieved when I don't swoop on this but view it with the same interest as I would other aspects of their life experience. What is important is that this and any other material can come into the room and not be left in the shadow.

I think of various male clients who have brought homoerotic feelings that were at the edge of their awareness into the work. The one was determined to bring this material but was aware of a sense of shame and difficulty in doing so.

It is good if a diversity of sexual experience can be included within the therapeutic space. Within one person, there is usually great diversity. Particularly in our homophobic world, it is good to acknowledge and welcome this richness.

In South Africa, where I work, we are also blessed by great cultural diversity. Some people are very comfortable in their skins – in this sense also in the colour of their skin – and for others it's hard, particularly given our history of *apartheid* where privilege was based on skin colour.

Tessa was brought up in what she regards as a typical coloured family, in a community where there was a lot of drinking and little emphasis on academic achievement. Her happiest time was a period spent in London where she felt she was not regarded as coloured but perhaps seen as being Brazilian or Spanish. I would encourage Tessa to re-claim her coloured identity and offer her the names of people who were doing work around this theme – strong vibrant coloured women in our local area. But Tessa would have none of this and I think perhaps I was wrong. Perhaps she just didn't want to identify in any way with this community in South Africa and that was that.

Vuyikazi came to see me. She was now in her 30s, had left an abusive relationship and was in

Cape Town bringing up her two daughters. Her father and mother were in another part of the country. Her mother treated her very harshly. Her parents had expected her to stay in her abusive marriage. They had married her off very young. It had seemed to her that her parents had wanted the bride price that would be paid for her hand in marriage. (The family was extremely poor.) She was furious about this.

Then Vuyokazi returned to her familial home in the countryside for a visit and, seemingly inadvertently, her one brother blurted out that her mother was not her mother at all. Her own mother, he explained, had died in her infancy. The woman she considered her mother was in fact her stepmother.

Rather than being angry, Vuyikazi was so relieved at this huge piece of history being revealed. It all made sense to her now. And to my surprise, rather than being angry with her stepmother, she was now appreciative of all this woman had done for her – Vuyikazi praised this woman for clothing and feeding her. She showed an amazing ability to move on and stopped seeing me soon after that.

There is a particular embodiment in indigenous

African women (and men) that western people don't commonly share without doing substantial work. There is a solidness. I attribute this to attuned early child-rearing. I sense that many black people are able to move through trauma in a cleaner way than people of my demographic.[119]

Perhaps it is also worth sharing work I did with groups of women (several men were in the groups too) who were employed in working-class communities, counselling people who were being tested for HIV/AIDS. The counsellors themselves lived in these same communities. We would meet in a rather large group – maybe eight people – for two hours once a month. It was a chance for the counsellors to talk about their work but many would also use the opportunity to process trauma in their own lives. I remember Nozipho entering the room and it was as if a gust of shock came in with her. It was only much later in our time together that day that she shared that two of her brothers had been imprisoned on account of a mob justice incident that had happened in the area where they lived. (Such incidents are tragically not uncommon at present and are a sign of severe societal breakdown.) But as she spoke, she was able to process some of the shock of this.

In another session, the counsellor Mabulara spoke of how a group of men had broken down the door of her brother's home at about one o'clock in the morning. Her brother's wife had pushed herself against the door to try to prevent the assailants from entering. The men entered, stole the flat-screen TV and in the process, the woman was shot dead – in the presence of her three young children. But as Mabulara told the story, with the group of us present to her pain and the horror of this assault which was still very fresh in her experience, there was a sense that even then some healing began. For me, this is extraordinary and it speaks of the health and resilience of black Africans, many of whom have received sensitive parenting and continue to offer this to their babies.

Do different cultures have particular woundings? I think this is surely so. I am most familiar with the woundings that present in people like me – people with an ancestry from England or Europe. Can people from different cultures work effectively with one another? I think so. And it may also be good, as with gender, to work with someone whose identity is more obviously similar to your own, at least for a while.

Reflection:

If these stories have shocked you – and they are extremely shocking – please go and have a cup of tea or take a walk outside.

What is your approach to difference? It is easily feared. Could you become more curious about difference of all kinds? How might you experiment with this?

Identity/labels

There is much talk these days on the question of identity. The question that is often posed is: how do you see yourself, how do you name your identity?

It took me some time to understand what was meant by identity. I'm not sure if I understand it yet. It is tricky territory. It can be empowering to claim an identity – for example that of being gay – but this very identity can then begin to hem you in and constrain your life and your experience of yourself.

Similarly, this applies to the labels that abound in the practice of psychology and psychiatry. What is it like to be called schizo-affective? I hear that for some people a label is welcomed. As though people can then relax a bit and think: oh, okay, this is why I experience life as I do. Even where this is the person's experience, I regard it as important for the health practitioner to hold much more than this label in their work with the person.

As a South African, I am delighted – and in a way

also saddened – by reading, as I have done a few times now, of people who don't identify as black. Chimamanda Ngozi Adichie, in an article entitled *Truth is no stranger to fiction,* writes:

> I remember clearly when I became black – in a gathering of friends, in an apartment, sitting around a wooden table with my Nigerian friend and her Chinese friend and her Japanese friend and her African-American friend and his Irish-American friend. In the middle of a conversation, one of them referred to me as black, and I realised that I had taken on this new, odd identity. It has stayed with me ever since, that scene.[120]

And in Jonny Steinberg's *A Man of Good Hope,* the lead character, the Somalian Asad, is in conversation with a local South African, and the South African refers to black people, including Asad in this.

Asad stared back at the old man in astonishment.

> 'Brother,' he tells me [Jonny]. 'I never thought I would see the day I am

described as black.'

He returned the old man's stare. 'I am not black,' he said sternly. 'I have my own culture.'

The old man laughed: not his usual quiet chuckle, but an open-throated, mirthful guffaw. 'When you are here in South Africa,' he said... 'you are black.'[121]

Mark Gevisser talks of claiming a gay identity in his book, *Lost and Found in Johannesburg*. It was a suit that didn't really fit, he said.[122]

I'm sorry we have to wear suits that don't fit. Our identities are so much more nuanced and mysterious than that. Of course, gay women and men also contain 'straight' identities within them, and vice versa. Why are people surprised when a gay man sleeps with a straight woman? We're not all one thing or the other. What malady is this that makes us clutch at labels? I know it is often part of a process of empowerment but it may well need discarding after a time. Ideally, our world would be one where labels weren't needed at all. After all, they say the word homosexual only came to

Presence in Relationship

Africa during colonisation. A name wasn't needed before – though this practice of love was widely accepted.

So here too we bring awareness and the sense of emptiness. Identity may be a form. But it need not be a fixed form. It can move and change and it is also always empty.

Reflection:

Does anything in this section leave you uncomfortable? If so, can you put your finger on why?

Is identity something you have had to grapple with? If so, how does the suit fit? Would it be good to step out of it, even just for a while?

Intergenerational wounding

That there is wounding that is carried down through the generations is quite clear to me from my own experience and that of my clients. This isn't bad news. It means too that healing can extend back to the generations that came before.

Familial and ancestral information is passed down to us in a mysterious non-cognitive way. So while we may not know the historical details, we might be playing out a sense of shock or the holding of a family secret unwittingly as it is part of the field that we now inhabit. There is more than the personal that enters the therapy room. At some level, we might be processing a collective experience of suffering, particularly if we or our ancestors lived at a time of national or global conflict. We may be baffled as to the cause of our suffering and this can be because it may be more than personal.

This is not territory that is easily given to understanding. But from my experience, it seems to me that one can process at least a little of the suffering that has gone before. This would resonate with some African understandings of the ancestral field. It is as if in bringing awareness to our own process, we also then transform some part of what has gone before.[123]

Family constellations is the name of a powerful modality where, in a group, an individual is invited to present a particular family scenario and members of the group then form a constellation representing the different people in the picture.

My uncle Mike had died and I attended a constellation to try to work with some of the mucky family stuff that had surfaced during his illness and death. The long tall man dressed in white who played my uncle quite soon exited the group and returned to his seat. Typical Mike, I thought, not wanting to deal with his feelings. Someone was asked to lie on the floor. It emerged that this person represented my dad who had been dead since I was 13. When the facilitator asked the person playing my dad how he was feeling, he responded: 'I'm like a slab.' It turned out he meant he wasn't feeling anything. Some work proceeded in the group with the person playing the 13-year-old me showing visible distress. Another woman – perhaps representing my older sister – tried to comfort her. When the brief constellation ended, my 'father' was asked how he felt now, and he responded: 'I am at peace.'

I remained bothered by part of what had happened and was helped by meeting up with one of the facilitators as I was washing my tea cup.

'I can't figure why my uncle just pushed off,' I remarked. 'He knew it had nothing to do with him,' responded the facilitator. That was helpful. From this, I surmised that all the emotions that were flying around with my uncle's illness and death were in fact matters that had remained unresolved from my father's death so many years before.

Similarly when I held an event in my home using the constellation method and called to mind my paternal granddad Albert – who I had never met – there was a palpable sense of shock in the room.[124] (One gets to know this quality.) One person found herself being extremely itchy all over. I think she was playing the role of Albert. He had died in the battle of Jutland in the First World War. His ship had been attacked and he drowned in the sea at night. It was as if the shock of this was still needing to be processed.

This can all seem very mysterious. Indigenous cultures know far more about this territory than those of us who consider ourselves educated and, therefore, not superstitious!

It can be helpful to be open to the possibility that the pain one is experiencing might not be all one's own. One may also carry some of the material of a nation. This would be particularly so for those of us who have lived in countries in trauma. Addressing this territory, Maura wisely says: 'Maybe only a little can be transformed. I can just work with what I'm given.'[125] We don't have to pay the price for all the pain and guilt of previous generations.

As ever in the work, one brings awareness to what arises. There is no need to desperately figure out whose wounds are whose, though some clarity may be helpful to the person. And sometimes the person may need to try to get additional information to help him/her understand what he/she is experiencing. For example, it may be helpful to know details about the conditions and effects of war on a particular town where a person's parents lived.

This is very much a joint enquiry. I have said to a client: 'Let's not try and find a quick answer. Let's find our way in this territory together.' There is no other way. It's a strange land. It's as if you are looking around together with your client to explore a landscape that may have some familiarity but is also very strange. As in the rest of the work, we need to respect the mystery.

I will return here to the client who had experienced a sense of being dumped on by all the trauma in her family on both her mother and father's side. She had been doing some reading in this area, and learnt of the term 'morphic resonance' that was popularised by Rupert Sheldrake. This too speaks of a field that holds more than the personal. So the individual may experience guilt, shame or shock and not understand why these feel so huge. It may be that, at least in part, these are from previous generations. Paula, in struggling with the injunction from another practitioner to 'let go' and walk away from this ancestral territory, rather came to see that if it works the one way, it works the other way too. This felt an important – and true – insight. So in working on herself, Paula is clearing the field, as it were, and sending health and healing to her ancestors in ways we may never fully understand. I sense this may be a turning point for her – though of course there is never really just one turning point. This insight allowed her to do the following ritual:

Paula: I found objects that meant a lot to them. I thought: What would comfort them? For my mom, it was the old visiting card of her brother. It was a bit brown with age, but otherwise perfect. For my father, it was a napkin that his mother had embroidered – very fine embroidery – as part of her dowry. She had died of tuberculosis when he was eight. He adored her. I found a photograph of my parents – which I usually keep well out of sight – and wrapped the photograph with the objects in the napkin.

Susan: Did you pack it like a bundle? [Making a round shape with my hands.]

Paula: No, I packed it more like a parcel, so that the object of comfort and peace would be close to each of them. So my mother was very close to her brother and my father had the embroidery of his mother touching him. I then took a piece of sacred red cord I'd been given that had come from a friend's visit to a high lama. And I tied this around the bundle and put it in a little drawer in an old piece of furniture of my mother's that she loved.

I like to think of her parents now resting with their most loved person in the parcel tied with the sacred cord. Work is being done in that drawer.

Reflection:

Do you have a response to this section? Do you perhaps dismiss it all as un-provable and so nonsense?

If you open yourself to this territory, is there anything that stirs in you?

Is there a conversation that it might be useful to have in your family of origin that has been sparked off by reading this?

Climate change

Climate chaos. Climate justice. These phrases sound more accurate than the rather innocuous sounding *climate change*.

We are altering our seasons. I am sad about this. Seasons form such a wonderful rhythm. What will it mean to live without these?

Climate justice is a useful term as the impact of climatic change is mostly felt by people – many of them in Africa – who rely on subsistence farming for an income. This livelihood is threatened when the rains don't come as expected, and when there are floods, when it does rain, that destroy crops. It is women who suffer the most as they work the land and feed their children.

A talk was advertised with the title *Is humanity committing suicide?* It seems quite clear to me that we are. If an individual pursues activities that will slowly kill them, we would regard this as un-wise at least. And we would probably create laws to make it more difficult for them to do this – thus we limit where people can smoke, increase the cost of cigarettes and so on. Vandana Shiva, the eco-activist from India, talks of us all as suffering from mental illness. Well, one can reasonably say that of people who are wilfully contributing to their own destruction. Maura, in speaking of what she refers to as mind-training in the West, says that we are trained in things that are unhelpful.[126] Hence the need for a return to, really, our right minds.

I had hoped that I would return to South Africa after my studies in England and do all the right things – install solar power, go off the grid, and so on. Not much of this has happened though my garden is slowly developing.

I sense my contribution will be in other ways. We each contribute from who we are. So perhaps my contribution may be towards helping us learn to live with each other better. This will be an essential skill as the waters rise.

I remember that before leaving England, I went to speak to Stephen Harding, a well-known ecologist based at the Schumacher College in the south of England.

'Stephen, I'll be living in a house in coastal Cape

Town – do you think it will be worth investing in it? How soon do you think before it'll be under water?' He took a look at me and said: 'Not in your lifetime, I don't think. The challenges will rather be food security and the resultant social insecurity.'[127] He seemed a bit amused by my question. To me it was entirely obvious and pragmatic. If I was going into a war zone, I'd be asking serious questions before setting up home there. I think the war analogy is a good one – unfortunately. It gives some extent of the 'all-over-ness' of the problems we will face. In fact, war is a gentle analogy relatively speaking. Climate chaos doesn't end I don't think.

This topic can get quite heavy and one can easily slide into a sense of guilt. Having lived in the first transition town, Totnes, in the south of England, I am aware that one can adopt a joyful approach to this crisis. I resonate with the information I received through them on the latest book by Charles Eisenstein, *The More Beautiful World our Hearts know is Possible*:

> In the face of grave ecological and social crisis, why is a spirit of optimism poking through the despair? And what's love got to do with it?

Yoga? Music? Or are these just distractions from the struggle at hand? Join Charles for a heady exploration of hope, naiveté, and the expansion of the realm of the possible.[128]

The Transition movement is working towards living beyond fossil fuels – hence the term transition. There is a lot of emphasis on fun and re-learning to do things our grandparents could do – re-skilling they call it – such as darning and repairing bike punctures. From another of their mailings on the book, *Occupy Love*:

Join acclaimed director Velcrow Ripper on a journey deep inside the revolution of the heart that is erupting around the planet, as he asks the question, 'How could the crisis we are facing become a love story?'

Carl Jung in a YouTube clip[129] says: 'If you think along the lines of nature, then you think properly.'

Chodron speaks similarly:

Times are difficult globally; awakening is no longer a luxury... It's becoming critical... The earth seems to be be-seeching us to connect with joy and discover our innermost essence. This is the best way that we can benefit others.[130]

One of my colleagues in England (from the Core Process community) offers a personal development retreat entitled *Fun and Games*. She says:

> Did you know that our ancestors dedicated a lot more energy to play than we do today? Communities of hunter gatherers spent around four hours a day on work. The remainder was dedicated to playing and games. Today, the evidence shows that play is just as vital for adults as it is for children as it connects us to a deeper place within ourselves as well as connects us to others.[131]

Yes, one can feel almost obliged to be 'heavy' in talking about climate change. Perhaps we can dare to trust that there's some huge creativity at play. And that it is in this that we can trust. I've sensed for a while that we'll *sing* the planet right!

Reflection:

What is your gut feeling on reading this? Fear? Anger? Denial? Whatever it is, can you sense it in your body? Maybe stay with it for a moment.

What do you feel about singing the planet right? Can you sense this has a different impact in the body?

PART
4

Approaching shock and trauma

It feels right that it is only now that we approach the territory that can rather alarmingly be called shock and trauma. In client work too it can be useful if this material does not come in too early so that a sense of trust and settledness has been established between the client and therapist.

This material is approached in the same way as the rest of the work. With gentleness and respect. But I am well aware that just naming this territory can put many of us on some kind of alert. We need not fear.

Current thinking on trauma is going through huge changes – thankfully. Health practitioners used to feel that after a shocking experience such as an assault or a car accident, one should receive counselling as quickly as possible. Now it is considered wiser to support the person, keep them safe, but leave at least a few days before offering a space for them to talk about their experience should they wish to do so. Research now shows that repeating the story of what has happened may in fact be re-traumatising. And, of course, we all know of times when we or others have needed to repeat – seemingly endlessly – the account of what has happened to us. So there can be no pre-scription here.

The Core Process approach to shock and trauma is informed by the accessible work of Peter Levine.[132] Let me begin with Levine's most instructive story (in my own words):

> There is a young deer grazing on an African plain. The deer gets the scent of lion on the air and moves into an alert stance. If the lion moves away, you will see the deer relax and continue grazing. But should the lion make chase, the deer runs for its life. If it manages to escape, once it is safe, if you watch, you will see it shaking. It is literally shaking the ter-ror out of its body, its nervous system. After this is complete it returns to graz-ing. All is well. If, however, the deer is caught by the lion, it will typically freeze. This is an instinctual response. The lion knows, also instinctively, that feeding on a dead animal may be poisonous. So

Presence in Relationship

the lion may now let go of the deer and move away. Should you be watching, you will slowly see the deer return from its numbed state and it will then go through its cleansing/shaking process.

This story is helpful as it tells us that recovering from shock is natural. We *know* how to heal from trauma. However, we may often need more support in this than the deer. When trauma is well met, we heal. We can move through traumatic events with little or no harm being done.

I went walking with my older sister and her toddling granddaughter. Towards the end of the walk, she came face to face – they were just about the same height – with a ridgeback dog. I can't remember what the dog did, but the little girl was shaken and startled and cried bitterly for a few moments. She was well met in this. No one said 'don't cry' or 'don't be silly'. She was held and comforted. It must've been scary. Within minutes she was on her way, amazing me as she had that day, at how fast a two-year-old can move.

You give full attention and then move on.

It is good to be aware of this shaking reflex as a

person heals from earlier experiences of shock. One of my clients who has had a particularly harrowing life has, on more than one occasion, shaken fairly uncontrollably during a session. The one time it was very pronounced. 'What is happening to me?' he asked when the wave of shock had passed. It was important that I was not frightened by this and could give him some explanation of his experience. Healing is happening at the level of the nervous system. It is very useful – as an individual and as those who work therapeutically with others – to have an awareness of this territory so that one can meet such experience without fear. It doesn't happen often in the obvious way I have cited, but there are more subtle variants of this.

Reflection:

How is it for you as we enter this territory together?

Is there any sense of dread, fear? Did this change as you continued reading and read about a more natural approach to the subject?

Are there particular experiences that flash in your memory when we speak of trauma? If so, can you be gentle with yourself here?

Shock

I will try to say something about the term shock and how it may be experienced. It has a zzz quality – as though a subtle electric charge is going through the body. Some people experience it as a chill, a shudder, an icy feeling. Note that you may get a similar sensation but it may indicate a sense of excitement or another emotion. So the context is important. The word shock describes it well. The sense is similar, I suppose, to the body receiving an electrical shock. The impact is on the body. And it's the body that often holds the key to healing. Trauma leads to a charged state and these energetic experiences need to complete. Adrenalin and other hormones get stored in the body – as in the example of the deer – but can be released even years after the traumatic event.

I'm not going to try to give particular definitions of shock and trauma. Sometimes I hear someone making a distinction between them that makes sense at the time but then I forget it again. And then I hear a different distinction between the two and that also sounds right. An absolute distinction between them may be false. We are referring to a sense sometimes referred to as overwhelm where the feeling I have is that my life is threatened. (This may not be the case, but it feels as though it is.)

Shock is strange in that we're not always aware that we're experiencing it. It may be that it's only when we're in a safe situation – which will generally mean with another person – that we really feel the impact of an earlier experience. Let me give an example of this.

I visited Dartmoor prison once a week as part of the chaplaincy team and got to know Neil. He is tall and attractive and has pictures of the Buddha and other beautiful items in his very neat cell. He was one of only a few men who shared the story of their criminal activity with me.

> I was robbing a house. The home-owner, a youngish man, returned while I was there. We fought, tumbling about on the floor. The man turned out to be a police officer. When I met him in court a few months later, his hair had turned white.

This made a huge impact on Neil.

It was only a couple of weeks later as I sat with Margaret in supervision and found myself retelling this story that I began shaking and crying and I realised I'd been deeply shocked by his account and had no doubt picked up Neil's sense of shock. After a time – it doesn't take long – this subsided and I was alright. But it was instructive in that it showed me that sometimes one doesn't know how one is being impacted at the time. This is one of the reasons why regular supervision is so vital in any sort of work with people. And indeed why some level of support is probably advisable for most of us.

Reflection:

From my description of shock, do you have memories of this?

Have you had the experience of only recognising after an event that it had in fact been shocking? Do you have a way of recovering from these?

Working with shock and trauma

It has become quite commonly known that in the event of experiencing a trauma one may have the experience of leaving one's body. This is often referred to as dissociation. So one disconnects from one's body. It's a survival mechanism. We are extremely sensitive creatures. Walking upright, exposing our hearts, is no small thing!

Dissociation will sometimes be the automatic experience of a person being attacked or sexually assaulted. One may then split off from feelings and sensations held in the body as the body is too dangerous a place to be. Dissociating in this way can be an excellent strategy and profoundly right given the experience of the person at the time – as in the experience of the deer freezing. It is good if one can remove a sense of shame from this.

Dissociation can also be extremely subtle. Some people live in a somewhat dissociative state due to growing up without the sense of enough safety or confidence in their body and environment. Part of the trickiness is that dissociation can feel good and even quite euphoric. It can be a lifetime's enquiry for many of us to begin to notice and know when we dissociate. Working with a therapist who is competent in this area can be helpful.

I worked with Marie for a year and a half. When she was about six, her father's colleague had sexually assaulted her on the stairs of the complex where she lived with her parents. In such incidents, as for Marie, the real trauma comes when the person is not believed when they spontaneously share the experience with their beloved parents – in Marie's case, her mother. This is a deep injury.

Part of my one session with Marie went as follows:

Marie: I'm in an ice block.

Susan: Is all of you in the ice block?

Marie: No, not my hands and feet.

Susan: Can any part of you move?

Marie: Yes, my eyes.

Where the client is reporting a sense of freezing,

it can be useful to ask where in the body there is movement, aliveness, as I did spontaneously in my enquiry with Marie. In the territory of shock and trauma, it's very useful – and essential I feel – to include the body in the work.

I remember one of my tutors sharing about a short conversation with her client:

Therapist: Where are you now?

Client: I'm on the ceiling.

Therapist: Can I join you there?

I like to think of the ensuing conversation as they hang about on the ceiling.

If there's a sense of the person hardly being in the room at all, one might sometimes ask: 'How far away are you?'

So with dissociation one enquires into the person's experience of not being particularly present in their bodies in the same way as one would enquire into other bodily sensations; one does not make the experience 'wrong'.

In the example I cite from working with Marie, the session moved along and I imagine later – or before the close of the session – I would have checked with her as to whether she was now feeling more present in her body. I hope this illustrates that the body can be included in a matter-of-fact simple kind of way, be given respect and gentle attention, and the session moves on. This does not lessen its profundity.

Working with a client who is reporting historical trauma, it may not be necessary for the client to relate all of a story. (Remember what I said earlier about the possibility of this being re-traumatising.) In the case of Teresa who I mentioned earlier – who twisted the pastry for jam tarts – I may say something like: 'You don't need to tell me the whole story. Just a headline may be enough for today.' Sometimes even just mentioning the intention to approach certain territory is enough. I might then ask: 'What comes up for you now that you have said you are going to speak about this today?' We would then touch into any impact in the body, or fear that may have arisen at the very thought of approaching the subject. This may well be enough for that session. An ability to stay at the edge of the difficulty can be empowering, returning to the person a sense of choice and some control.[133]

A client may report a great sense of tiredness that has overcome them. This may be related to some huge responsibilities they have at present, such as caring for a sick parent. Or it may be that something of a more emotional or spiritual nature is, as it were, pressing on them and resulting in their great weariness. It is good here to just bring awareness to the sense of tiredness, and perhaps explore where it is experienced in the body. Mysteriously once acknowledged in this way, it may move along on its own.

Shock and trauma are curious territories as they can be rather unpredictable. An event that you might expect to prove overwhelming is not. And something you feel should be quite minor – like getting a little bump in the car – may somehow throw you into great panic and fear. We know now that periods of hospitalisation and surgery – particularly as a child – can be highly traumatising. Whether the trauma is in the nature of what might be regarded as an everyday bruise or something more sharp and startling, each is in need of respect and recognition.

In working with shock and trauma, the person in the room is accessing past history within the body-mind system as though the historical event

Presence in Relationship

was happening now. They are experiencing the shock and overwhelm that is still present within their system. It is with this that one is working. Historical wounding can be cleared and one does not have to live from that wounding although I would say a certain vulnerability may remain.

As in all the work, it is about awareness, enquiry and staying in the present moment. It involves being open to the impact of the work and not splitting off into one's head (as the therapist). One rests in resource and the *brahmaviharas*. One is not on one's own. This is vital.

In all of this, the therapist is offering a steady presence and a safe environment. This containment is essential if the client is to be adequately met in this difficult space. This is important work. Clearing these areas of trauma frees things up for the client. And working with trauma is not necessarily discrete and separate from the rest of the work one is doing. One can be dealing with trauma in the ordinary course of the work. We are probably all moving in and out of it in some way in the ordinary course of a day or an hour. But particularly where the material coming into the room is palpably charged with shock, the therapist needs to receive good support in the work. Let me stress again, supervision should not only be sought in a sort of emergency manner. Regular scheduled supervision is essential if the therapist is to grow in the work and for the client to be well-served. It is a necessary requirement of practice.

With good training, this territory of shock and trauma is in fact not difficult to meet. Staying present and grounded in yourself as practitioner is key when with a client in difficultly. Don't let the whole session be mega-intense. Don't require the client to change or even 'get better'. One is holding brilliant sanity and a deep confidence in the client's natural healing process (remember the deer?). An option always is not to go there. There is always the possibility of just touching very briefly on the matter, and then returning to resource, to safety. This is what I meant when I said it can be useful if being with trauma comes a bit later in the work once a relationship has been established. It is also good to know what the client's resources are and whether their lives are manageable. But often it seems the psyche knows when the person is ready to look at certain material.

Gentleness and slowness are crucial in this work. A simple hanging out at the edge, as it were, of the trauma may be more than enough – at least to start with. Letting the client know that you as therapist are okay in this territory can be useful, as the client can well imagine that her/his experience is too much for you. It's fine to actually tell the client this. I might say: 'You may be concerned about how I am. I'm glad to be with you in what you're experiencing right now.' Saying something like this (if it is true) indicates that you are not afraid of the territory the client is visiting. Strange as it may seem, humour can also be helpful, even in the form of taking a little break, as it were, in the course of what may be quite a heavy session. So I may say something like: 'Wow, this is quite hectic isn't it? Shall we take a short pause?' Light remarks like this can sometimes give a bit of breathing space to both the client and therapist.

One would generally seek to end the session with the client having recovered some ground if one was traversing this sort of territory together. S/he needs to be able to leave the room with enough sense of safety to move on to where they are going next – or to be encouraged to stop for coffee or a walk in the area.

Reflection:

How are you doing? You might yourself like to pause here and have a drink, stretch or walk around a bit before you continue reading.

The COEX system

Stanislav Grof, who with his wife Christina is a pioneer in the field of transpersonal psychology, speaks of what he calls the COEX system, COEX standing for condensed experience. It is useful to know about this.

Grof describes the COEX system as follows. You have a certain experience and that experience has a resonance with earlier experiences in your life. It is as if a C is struck on a keyboard and all the other Cs echo in resonance. Grof explains it thus:

> All of our history is held within present time in a layered and condensed fashion. The various layers of experience coalesce and generate various mind-body states and behavioural patterns.[134]

This helps to explain how perhaps a smallish experience can feel quite overwhelming. So for example, a sense of disappointment with a key individual at one's workplace can prove very upsetting and unsettling. It may be that this experience resonates with an earlier experience of profound disappointment – perhaps also with a senior person in one's history such as a parent or another relative or significant other. So there is an echo from earlier experience that is set off by the present experience and this magnifies the impact of the immediate incident. It can be useful to recognise this and, as it were, to uncouple the experiences. When I mention the COEX system to a client – and I sometimes do – there can be immediate recognition. And it may be that the person is interested but that there's no immediate 'fit'. A question I may ask is: 'Is this familiar?' This may enable the person to link back from the immediate experience to other events that have resonance with it and that have become coupled with their present experience.

We hold various COEX systems within us around different themes. Franklyn says examples of these may be abandonment or the loss of trust in intimacy. He notes that COEX systems also relate to positive experience and there can for example be condensed experience echoes that support our self-worth. This is good to know and to build on.

Reflection:

Does reading of the COEX system remind you of so-called small events that have loomed large for you? Might this provide some explanation for it?

Recognising shock and trauma

How do we slowly learn to recognise this territory in ourselves and others and bring it to awareness? It takes time.

Maura encouraged us to learn how to recognise shocked states in ourselves as well as in our clients. She helpfully shared signs that she has learnt that indicate to her that she's no longer okay. I found this extremely helpful in my own enquiry. She mentioned the following factors:

- A furious response, becoming very oppositional;

- A sense of disturbance in my eyes – what she described as flickering eyes;

- Getting migraine symptoms;

- Going into my head and there being lots and lots of words and stories about the matter. Compulsive thinking and rethinking of a situation;

- A sense of spaciness;

- Sensations around the stomach and solar plexus;

- I basically don't feel good. I can't function and

- A certain sensation around my throat.[135]

These are things that typically arise in everyday life but we kind of carry on regardless. It can be useful if one can begin to notice these sensations – even if they present in quite a subtle way. Offering yourself compassionate interest and checking in with yourself as to whether you're doing okay is good to do.

Maura says that she knows something is going on for her by her response. It is useful to get to know one's own signs of shock or overwhelm – when things are too much. It is good to respect one's reaction, to pay attention to it and perhaps to find a way of mediating or soothing this. Sometimes just the recognition is enough.

One does not need to know why the particular feeling or sensation arises or seek for a story behind it. On occasion as I'm leaving the house, I feel unsettled – lately this manifests in an unease in my belly. I try to give this sensation a little time – if I am able to do so. And on occasion I leave what I was about to do and just stay home. Of course this isn't always possible.

We may notice that we are drawn to crises, to drama and intensity, as this is what we are familiar with. We can become used to living life rather on the edge – that is, not in a very resourced place. It can be quite hard to see this and slowly begin to address it. Again, working with a therapist can be helpful here.

Shock and trauma, as we have seen, can have a very strong energy. It can knock us off our feet and we can get lost in it. It can cause us to spiral down and we can assume the re-living of the difficulty is helpful. Rather, what can be useful is to slow the whole process down. So simple phrases that may be used are: 'Take your time here', 'Can we just pause for a moment?', or 'Shall we slow this down a bit?' Pausing, braking, this can be the territory. It is not that one is trying to move away from the material. One is rather giving it space. This slowing down, though some people won't welcome it, is essential – for the client *and* the therapist really.

One can't go into trauma with the same energy of trauma – one has to bring something different to it.

And let me remind you again that trauma doesn't always manifest in a dramatic way. It can be the so-called little snub that can destabilise a person. It can be the everyday bruises as much as the larger more dramatic events of life that call for our care and respect.

I like to always have flowers in the room and these often prove to be a resource when working in rather difficult territory. Apart from the sheer beauty, a person may also like to, for example, rub the lavender in the arrangement and get the fresh scent of the plant as their way of moving to resource and goodness. This would be a creative way of pausing in the session.

When the client is in difficult territory, processing a strong memory or with a sensation in their body that they don't understand, it is important that they know that they are not alone, that they are no longer without the support they once sorely needed.[136] Sometimes I say things like: 'You're feeling threatened but you are safe now.' One is keeping a sense of present time though being impacted by the client in their distress. Verbal contact may be important so that the client can know your presence.

I have noted elsewhere that being willing to explore questions, such as what anchors and comforts one, can be complicated for the person who may have had a long history of stress and fear.[137] This work can be extremely delicate –and essential.

When there is a sense of the client being overwhelmed or in shock, a response that Franklyn calls the orienting response, is useful. This may include simply encouraging the person to look around the room or notice a flower arrangement. Making contact with the floor by placing one's hands or feet on the floor or making contact with the arms of the chair can increase a sense of grounding. One helps the person to be present and stays in contact with them. Part of the earlier experience of trauma is that the person was unsupported and alone. In a therapeutic session, he/she is no longer alone.

There may be signs that one is entering the territory of shock and trauma. Things to look out for are:

- A sense of things speeding up. The person may be talking very quickly, with little space between sentences. There is a sense of speed and little space;

- Freezing. The person may report a sense of numbness;

- Dreaminess, a sense of the person being far away. This is something one can sense even if the client does not remark on this themselves. The therapist may experience this as a sort of blurring in her own vision;

- A change in the colouring of the person. The person may suddenly become very pale. This would be hard to miss. I may remark on it to the client if we have worked together for a while. Otherwise I would note it and take special care in the session;

- The person may report a change of temperature – that they are suddenly cold or hot – or move between different temperatures;

- Breathing and heart rates may change and either the therapist or the client may notice and report on this; and

- When people report sensations in their eyes this may be a sign of there being shock in the field.

Let me end this section with a few more examples.

So changes in a person's colouring and even markings on the body can arise in the therapeutic process. Noticing such physical changes can alert the practitioner that the client may be accessing a traumatic memory, as in the following example:

As Margaret and I sit on the floor on supportive chairs facing each other, something changes for a moment. I notice how she drops her face to the side and looks paler, as if she is losing her vitality. It is very different from how she has been in the session up until now.

Susan: What's happening now?

Margaret: I'm remembering how I was left in hospital when I was about 18-months-old. My mother left me. She couldn't stay as my four-month old sister was at home. There wasn't a policy then that parents should stay with their children. That only came in later. We were immigrants and poor. She didn't have the money to ask someone to care for my sister. I went into a sort of moribund state, out of contact with everything.

This is what I'd seen in her face at that moment.

Margaret: When she came back I didn't want to respond to her. It took a while.

In this instance, I think I did later mention to Margaret how her appearance had changed. She did not seem to find this disturbing as it resonated with her experience during the session.

Another client related a hair-raising ordeal, experienced while driving on a mountain pass with her two infants in the car and a huge lorry behind them. As she spoke, she developed markings on her forehead which was the area of injury from the accident that ensued. I remember clearly how, as she spoke, a large truck pulled up directly outside the window of the room where we were meeting in a small rural town. This was something that had never happened before nor did it happen again.

One learns to recognise shock and trauma in oneself and others. It's a bit, I suppose, like learning a new language. In the next section we will look at how we can meet ourselves and others in this space of difficulty.

Reflection:

How are you doing now?

In noting these different possible pointers to recognising shock and overwhelm, are any of them familiar to you? Do you have anything to add?

Breathe if you need to.

Holding health and difficulty

How does one meet a person – or indeed oneself – when in trauma or shock? I have given some indications in the previous sections. Here I deal with the importance of what can be called holding health and difficulty. This is a key skill to develop.

I have mentioned that trauma can have something of a magnetic quality. It pulls one in, filling the space so that nothing else is noticed. This is why returning to the body is useful. We have a tendency to follow what is difficult. Part of the makeup of our brain that we share with animals is on the alert for danger. Some people do not welcome being invited away from the tug of the traumatic material – even for a moment. The skill here is to be aware of the trauma and something else. The trauma is never all there is.[138]

Donington stresses that:

> It is important that clients don't feel overwhelmed by opening up threatening territory... too quickly. Defences are there for good reason.[139]

Defences often get bad press but they should be delicately respected. They will fall away when they are no longer needed.

In the midst of difficulty – in life or in a therapy session – one might ask the key question: What helps? And sure, sometimes help just can't be found.

In the therapeutic space, what can help to slow things down and allow space and resource? Franklyn uses the term titration – a term drawn from chemistry – in his teaching on trauma. The chemical process is one where one drops a certain chemical into another substance drop by drop by drop. This gives a sense of the fineness of the process. This is how one works with trauma. Little bit by little bit.

Giving the person permission and encouraging them to work slowly may be seen by the client as novel. It can be moving to be told by your therapist, in a gentle and kind voice: 'You can take your time'. What a gift these few words can be. I remember in the training, a colleague saying these words to me in a practice session we were doing together and I've never forgotten them. There's time!

I have said that there is something about the nature of trauma that makes the person almost compulsively want to run headlong into it. It can be quite hard to put the brakes on this. One client becomes openly annoyed with me when I suggest: 'Okay, Ashraf, that may be enough difficulty for one day'. 'Why do you try to stop me?' he asks angrily. 'I want to know the truth!' It may be a sign of health when he is willing to rest quietly and know that, yes, this has been enough for one day. But equally, I need to keep attuning to his innate health and wisdom.

Franklyn speaks of what he calls the trauma vortex. This describes the sense of getting sucked down into the traumatic material. And he speaks of the usefulness of then building up a countering healing vortex. This may be resisted by the traumatised client.

The healing vortex is developed by encouraging the client to learn to rest in spaces and activities that are soothing, that don't activate him/her. To build up a repertoire, as it were, of safe spaces – within or outside of oneself. Are there places one can return to when the going gets tough? This is a huge skill and not one we're accustomed to value in our society. It's as though struggling and being in difficulty is somehow more valid than living a life that's quiet and peaceful. While one may build this healing vortex quite deliberately, more often it is a subtle part of the ongoing work where one notices areas of ease for the client, points out where there is an absence of difficulty, and so on. It takes time.

Franklyn refers to another skill he calls uncoupling. Traumatic material can feel as though it's one big chunk. Uncoupling involves dealing with pieces of the trauma in small bits rather than trying to cope with it all at once. It may mean delinking various incidents that the client had considered together but are in fact discreet from one another.

I have explained that in times of stress, the whole system of layered experience can arise together and be overwhelming for the person. The work here is to use the skill of uncoupling to help the layers that have condensed together to uncouple and to work with one thing at a time.

It is an extremely useful skill to be able to bring oneself back from a place of overwhelm. (I find it isn't always possible for me and will take a life-time of practice.) This is a skill that can be learnt in the therapeutic space. If you become lost and are drowning in painful memories, you can be helped to know that, now, in real time, you are safe. If you have been attacked in the past, the attacker is no longer present. Remaining in the present moment is extremely important for the therapist and this enables the client to return to the present. Again, staying grounded and resourced is a key therapeutic skill. I can't emphasise this enough. And this does not mean one is not affected. It's shaky work for both the client and the therapist.

The healing vortex is the place that one seeks to strengthen with the client during the course of the work. A place of security, of okay-ness. It is simply no good as the therapist to focus only on the difficulty – even if this is what the client is doing. Other writers have referred to this as touch and go. You touch into the difficulty and then return to resource. This movement to and fro is a skilful one and can be done in a subtle way that may not be obvious. It can be empowering for the client to know that they can choose to move away from difficulty. Clients who have been severely traumatised may, as I have mentioned, resist this resting in health. The trauma space has become their familiar ground. And there can be a sense, understandably, of being determined to 'crack' this (whatever the 'this' is). A gentle and gradual approach is needed. One is supporting the natural healing process and creating a deeper healing container for the pain.

Let me add that in working with trauma in Core Process – as in some other modalities – restoring an accurate memory of events is not necessary and indeed is often impossible. The memory may have a tone to it rather than words as it may have happened before the person had language. Hence the title of Babette Rothschild's book, *The Body Remembers*. The perpetrator may have died and so not be available to be confronted to confirm or deny one's experience. To try to secure a clear cognitive memory would be a linear approach. Rather, the truth of the event is present in the room. I can truly attest to the fact that the body remembers, although I may not be able to explain the mystery of the mechanisms by which this happens. So the particular historical details may not be able to be precise and this does not necessarily matter. Some people will want to research and find as much detail as they can. This may be what they need to do and one would then support them in this.

Rothschild, who uses the term resources and anchors interchangeably,[140] rather beautifully says that:

> The more resources the client has, the
> easier the therapy and more hopeful
> the prognosis... It is a good idea to be
> equally on the lookout for resources
> as for traumas.[141]

So one looks for signs of health in building the healing vortex. The practitioner is holding the brilliant sanity, the image-of-God-ness, of the person in front of them. In Core Process there is the invitation for the client to stay with what is good and to build the capacity for this. This may be very new for the person and not what they expect from psychotherapy. It is something that can be developed. One client made an almost passing reference to an enjoyment of singing which, when enquired into, revealed a deep passion for singing opera which also linked her with her deceased father. People in difficulty will typically overlook the positive. Building resilience for staying with goodness is part of the work. One lingers with goodness in the session, savouring it. As I've said, people often regard this as peculiar, as though surely it's only the messy stuff that is wanted in a psychotherapy session. Certainly not. An increased tolerance for goodness is a good sign. So even a simple exchange can be a lovely indication of a return to health, as in this extract from a session with someone who had it rough, to say the least:

Susan: [As the session was ending.] How was the session?

Joan: Interesting... [she said with a smile].

This was new.

Often the work needs slowing down as the nature of trauma can involve, as I have said, things speeding up and getting out of control. In the case of people having frozen, there may need to be a process of de-freezing, and finding motion again in the body. Then the question might be: 'What action would your body like to do now?' In trauma, often the action that was required could not be completed – such as kicking someone or running away. One can then help to support the client to plan the action and execute it slowly. Or he/she can imagine – in real detail – carrying out the action that they were not able to do at the time of the traumatic event.

Holding health and difficulty. Franklyn also teaches how this might be practiced in the body. This he refers to as shuttling. So one would sense into an area of difficulty in the body – any part of the

Presence in Relationship

body that is uneasy, in discomfort, something like that. One is then invited to notice a part of the body that feels alright, even good. If this place can be accessed, the person can then experiment with moving from the place of difficulty to the place of resource. This is a useful although not altogether easy skill to develop. Another form it may take would be to, from the place of difficulty, also include the place of resource – so that one is allowing both of these to be present. Shuttling is in a sense a metaphor for holding health and difficulty at the same time. It helps you know that the difficulty isn't the whole of you. That's important. (Even if part of you can't believe this.)

The sadness is that many of us are walking around in trauma and it's become our accepted way of being in the world. I think of men – now in mid-life – in South Africa who were conscripted into the all-white *apartheid* army where they were indoctrinated and forced to carry out atrocities against their fellow citizens. These men suffer from deep wounds that have not yet been recognised. This is no doubt the story of war survivors the world over. These compromised people then live their adult lives with the trauma still running them, resulting in crime, broken marriages and other relationship breakdowns. Many of us have our own version of this though it is perhaps less dramatic and with contributing factors that are less clear to us. I have mentioned that the trauma of parents and grandparents can also effect subsequent generations. The price to our societies is high.

In the territory of shock and trauma one works slowly and with respect. You work with pieces of difficulty at a time. It may be two years before some space opens up for the person. You feel the nature of your relationship change. The client who would always show her annoyance if you suggested she try and rest in things that were easy, is now able to hear you when you say:

> There's more ...a sense of space in the sessions now. You speak of your body feeling more at ease. Allow the goodness to be there. Don't try and work hard at things. Appreciate the goodness that's happening. Your nervous system is healing.

And this time, she smiles and doesn't argue.

Building resource is key. I have said before that we can learn much from indigenous societies.

While indigenous peoples still suffer terribly from the impacts of past exploitation... they can help the world because they still hold a deep and close connection to the land and because they understand the power of ceremony to create transformation.[142]

Though a different form, this is not far from the work that Core Process is offering.

Reflection:

How are you doing? Is this heavy going?

Do you recognise yourself in any of this? Take it easy if you do.

Do you have any sense of an anchor or resource that you can return to when in difficulty? How might you build or strengthen this? Does this sound silly?

Boundaries

Boundaries are vital in therapeutic work – and indeed in all relationships. And they can, for some of us, be difficult to hold.

For a time I worked with a movement therapist in England. When an hour was up – the agreed duration of the session – she would let the session overrun by about 10 minutes. This didn't work for me. At one level I could feel I was getting a good deal, but it threw me. I didn't know where I was. I asked her to keep the sessions to an hour and she did.

I have a warm loving friend who sees clients as a social worker. She must offer them so much. But she overruns by an hour sometimes. I tell her firmly that she can't do this. She's always, of course, overwhelmed by her work. She sees people in severe distress. Maybe even more reason to keep the time boundary firmly. An hour is enough for the therapist as well as for the client. There may be exceptions to this where one agrees with the client to have longer sessions – this may be the case if they live some distance away for example.

Presence in Relationship

But the general guidance is to keep to an agreed time boundary – and to negotiate together any change to this.

We all know of families where parents – at least in our opinion – aren't very boundaried with their children. These can be – and often are in my experience – the most loving of families. But the children are not well served by this. It seems there may be something in a person that makes them feel that placing a firm boundary is unkind. And perhaps others of us need to soften our boundaries somewhat. It's an interesting area of enquiry.

Sometimes I ask clients how they might image a boundary. For some it might need to be a firm wall at some point, if for example a person is negotiating distance from a former partner or something like that. At other times a boundary may be sensed as softer – somehow the image of soft green velvet comes to mind and I imagine the sort of long cushion people put under doors to keep the draft out. There's something here about the kindness of a boundary and its protective function. Perhaps the more important the relationship, the more attention the boundary requires?

Not transgressing the sexual boundary in therapy

and other relationships of trust is vital. And this isn't to say we should not welcome sexual energy entering the therapeutic space. I know this can feel quite dangerous and of course there is an edge to it. Here again supervision is important. The person who has been violated sexually may need to even be a bit seductive with the therapist. There may be a closeness he/she longs for. The therapist need not fear this. Some clients – I know because a friend did this – even ask their therapist whether they are sexually attracted to them.[143] Remember everything is welcome. So a situation that feels quite hot sexually may arise and may need to be tolerated by the therapist – possibly even enjoyed if the sense is that the client needs to be appreciated in this space. But what is vital is not acting on this energy. This is where the healing comes. The client realises that, yes, there are people with whom I can show vulnerability, even sexual availability, and they will not take advantage of me. Conversely, if yet again the client is violated, it is better – far better – that she had never begun to meet with that practitioner. And that person would hopefully be struck off the role of practicing psychotherapists – at least for a time.

Rees speaks of boundary with reference to the Sanskrit word 'sila':[144]

In therapy, '*sila*' is, for me, bound-ary. The word means to build a hedge around, and is all about holding, con-taining, safety, and right relationship. No simple thing, and in each session, each relationship, I need to re-visit it, finding new subtleties that need attention.

I have not dwelt much on confidentiality until now. This fits under boundary – and indeed it fits everywhere. There can be no effective work with-out it. The relationship with the client has a qual-ity of the sacred – it *is* sacred. In many ways, it is a ritualised relationship. It is contractual in that the practitioner is paid – usually quite well paid. Confidentiality is part of the contract. I remember saying to my own therapist that I'd be furious if he disclosed to anyone that I was seeing him. He immediately said that I'd be right to be furious. It is an absolutely bottom line ethic not to disclose that you are seeing someone, let alone to breathe the slightest hint of what happens in a session outside of a very specially constituted space such as supervision where, too, confidentially is pro-foundly respected.

Some of my colleagues find me a bit quaint in

this regard but I feel too many exceptions are made. An absolute rule is helpful for the practitioner. Even when talking to a trusted colleague, it is unwise to make any more than a very general remark about one's work. (Even this I'm unsure about.) Any reflections on the work need to happen in a very held and respectful environment where the conditions have been set up to receive such information.

There is an energetic boundary that also deserves mention here. In his work on trauma, Franklyn speaks of the danger of violating the client's energetic boundary. This happens very easily and often with the best intention – that of being available to the person you are with. As Franklyn says, many therapists subtly invade their client's system with their attention without realising it.[145] Perhaps you recognise this experience from when it has happened to you. A person can be either physically or energetically 'in your space'. It doesn't feel good at all and it complicates the relational field. Franklyn suggests simple exercises where one practises moving one's energy towards and then away from a person, inviting their feedback on what they experience. He says:

Presence in Relationship

> If your attention is too close or too distant, the quality of your relational field may not feel safe or contained.[146]

This is interesting and subtle work. The exercises I suggested in the section on paying attention can help one attend to this energetic boundary. Like everything else, it can be learnt.

Reflection:

What is your experience of boundary? Do you appreciate people who hold boundary quite firmly? What is your own tendency?

Do you have a sense of what is meant by holding an energetic boundary? Might you want to make any changes in how you work with your energy in relationship?

What is your take regarding confidentiality? Is it an area you could firm up on or are you satisfied with how you manage this in your relationships? Are you comfortable with the way this is offered to you by your significant others?

Character strategies

We have spoken of primary patterning in the section on the perinatal field. This covers the time from conception to just after birth, with the responses the child receives in this period contributing to an early patterning in the growing being.

Secondary patterning follows, covering the period from birth to the first five years. Donington explains that secondary patterning is built from our relationships with significant others during this period.[147] Character strategies belong to the realm of secondary patterning.

Mainstream psychology speaks of personality types and this would include borderline personality disorder, narcissistic personality types, and so on. In Core Process we speak of character strategies.[148] Perhaps you can sense how this phrase has a different tone. Character strategies are ways of being that we develop in response to certain deficits or wounding that we experience in the first five years of life. There is a wisdom in these strategies and they enable us to meet our environment in a way that doesn't overwhelm us. The strategies are protective, as the term suggests, and each has associated gifts which are included in the name of each strategy.

There are five character strategies, the first of which is sensitive/withdrawn. This I will describe in some detail. This strategy relates to the period from just after birth to six months. Different body types tend to accompany the different character strategies. So for the sensitive/withdrawn, the body structure is often long – a tall person. Often the person is slim with a sense of their energy being quite contained. There may be a sense of tenseness about the person. People with a pre-dominance of this strategy may tend towards isolation and may struggle to create and maintain relationships. The associated gifts for the sensitive/withdrawn include creativity and spirituality. These people are in a way living quite close to the unseen world.

The other four strategies are dependent/endearing (a response to the first two years of life), charming/seductive (eighteen months to two and a half years), burdened/enduring (two and a half to three and a half) and industrious/over-focussed (three and a half to four and a half).[149] It is also useful to note that while one strategy may predominate, usually there will also be hints of other strategies within one person. It may be useful not to fix ourselves too much in one particular category.

The naming of these characteristics as strategies rather than suggesting they are disorders is helpful. They are patterns that develop in response to the conditions we experience as a developing being. And they also hold emptiness. They can adjust and change. The tendency of our patterning may remain but we can bring awareness to this and so modulate how we live *with* rather than *from* it. And that each strategy has its accompanying gift is also so heartening.

Reflection:

I am just giving a hint of this territory. If it doesn't interest you, I don't feel it's essential to understand.

Self as process

We tend to see ourselves – and others – as fixed, rather than recognising that we are all in process all the time. This is something I love about Nelson Mandela's biography *Long Walk to Freedom*. You see clearly how he develops over time.

It can be empowering to feel the openness and possibility that this offers. Maura has said:

> Most of us are not fully met at the being level when we first need to be and we come to identify as a separate and fixed self.[150]

Buddhism is interested in how the self arises in the moment.[151] In this model, the 'self' is seen as a constellation of psycho-emotional and physiological processes that we generally identify as 'me' or 'myself'.[152] This is a mouthful of a sentence and may be worth re-reading as it has a wonder to it. So the 'form' of self has a certain porousness to it (Remember what we covered earlier about form and emptiness).

If one dwells on this a little, one can sense that it is indeed good news. It is this sense of fluidity and possibility that the Core Process psychotherapist holds. (It is less easy, in my experience, to hold it for oneself.) Franklyn has noted that:

> The self and its constructs may be sensed to be a process, rather than a thing. With this realization, space naturally arises. It may be directly perceived that our true nature is more open and whole than we may have ever imagined.[153]

He teaches how awareness can begin to open the cycling of what he calls the self-system.[154] He expresses this well when he says:

> When we enquire into our process, we can experience the deeper reality that what we sense to be our 'self' is only a continuous movement of mental, emotional and physical processes. This can open to a sense of expanded possibility, to a feeling of spaciousness within all of our experience, to participation in a much larger and interconnected consciousness... The idea

that we can experience that which goes beyond the personal self, and that this experience is deeply integrative and healing, lies at the heart of Buddhist psychology and Core Process Psychotherapy.[155]

Maura similarly states that:

What we usually understand by 'personality' is the end-point of a continuous process of 'becoming' of which we are not normally aware. Core Process Psychotherapy works by paying attention to this shaping process as it is happening right now, and bringing awareness to the way in which we hold onto our past experience in the present moment. The foundation of Core Process Psychotherapy is the belief and experience that awareness is, in itself, transformative and healing.[156]

It was this process of becoming that resulted in each of us having the self form we inhabit and which, as we've noted, we can experience as quite fixed. So too the process can be unwound. In the present moment we can be with our past conditioning, offer this spaciousness and interest and the self then reconstellates and changes little by little.

In Core Process you often hear the phrase 'following process'. As Donington says in the article that has been a useful resource in my writing:

> 'Following process' is a very permissive and gentle way of working, but it is also extremely powerful, and can release enormous charge... One potential pitfall can be simply to underestimate the depth of the work. [157]

So in therapeutic work one is very much with this sense that the person in front of you is shifting and changing and this is a mystery you are involved in together.

Real transformation is possible. Not just a shuffling around of things, but deep transformation. I see it in my clients and I see it in myself. And it takes time and love.

Reflection:

This section may be something you want to come back to at another time. I find it can hardly be taken in on first reading. Or perhaps your experience is different.

The cultivation of the psychotherapist

Core Process Psychotherapy offers a contemplative approach to relationship, to both oneself and others. A distinguishing factor is that it is designed to support and hold the practitioner equally with the client. This makes a big difference – to both parties.

In teaching I sometimes refer to a local organisation called Soil for Life. It took me a while to unravel that title, but then I saw that, right, it's all about the soil. If the soil is healthy, growth happens. (It is an organisation that teaches organic gardening.) So too with Core Process Psychotherapy. Here it is the practitioner who is being cultivated.

Maura speaks movingly of this in the published interview I have drawn on several times:

> Our training is nearly one hundred percent geared to the cultivation of the psychotherapist. Things are interconnected. The client's journey will be

assisted by the psychotherapist's ability to be present at greater and greater depths, and subtler and subtler places. If the psychotherapist cannot do this the client will be restricted. So the client's growth or movement will be determined by the psychotherapist's limitations.[158]

The practitioner needs to have an ongoing commitment to working with their own 'stuff'.

Maura has said elsewhere that the training is based:

> ...on re-sensitizing the practitioner to their human condition. As we sensitise ourselves to our own condition, we also become more sensitive to that of the client's.[159]

In the interview I have referred to, Maura is asked a question about the vulnerability of the psychotherapist and responds as follows:

> The psychotherapist has to be vulnerable [but] it's the vulnerability of the warrior as opposed to the vulnerability

of a vulnerable person. It is the ability to meet whatever is coming at them. It's about the capacity to hold, to take things personally and not personally at the same time.[160]

An appreciation of the mystery of this joint practice, says Maura, keeps the psychotherapist in the right relationship to the work.[161] Right relationship to the work. What a lovely consideration.

By the cultivation of the psychotherapist, Maura is talking of elements I have already covered. These include the following:

- resting in spaciousness, emptiness;

- embracing the territory of the *brahmaviharas*;

- attending to resourcing in one's own life;

- equipping oneself with training that allows one to undo the linear and cognitive habits of a lifetime to allow for an enquiry that is grounded in a more subtle field;

- being able to meet trauma in another with confidence and without fear;

Presence in Relationship

- bringing awareness to the arising process of the client;

- willingness to restrain the impulse to interpret, even to question, resisting your own curiosity at times; and

- following the client.

This is the territory – the soil for life. And the client grows.

Reflection:

I expect this section to be of particular interest to those involved in therapeutic work with clients. Do you sense a longing for a different paradigm? Or perhaps you recognise your own way of working here?

The impact of the work on the psychotherapist

The psychotherapist in the Core Process model is truly present in the work. S/he is not playing a role but is being fully herself. One is affected by the client and this is not considered to be *wrong*.

Maura puts it beautifully in *Licking Honey from the Razor's Edge*:[162]

> We are not one step removed. We are being fully available... The therapist is not the boss. There is a profound equality and integrity of relationship despite the apparent... need or disturbance of the client... There is no hiding behind the role as a psychotherapist.

I've found that mainstream psychology can tend to make everything the client's problem. Any feedback s/he gives the therapist can be interpreted as their own issue rather than being seriously considered by the therapist. This leaves the client in an impossible situation really.

Elsewhere Maura has said:

> As myself – Maura – can I allow my-
> self, here and now, to be affected by
> the client and not just say 'that's a
> projection, that is not my stuff. I don't
> have to bother with that'.[163]

It comes as a huge relief to clients when the therapist is real.

Reflection:

Any wry smiles on reading this – from clients or
therapists? Any response of relief from clients or
would-be clients?

When good things happen

This is an area that may not have been given due attention in psychotherapy.

Melissa has a doctorate in physics and has done post-doctoral research and writing. She has a hugely original mind and was looking for a way of living that was out of the mainstream of her discipline. Suddenly she was approached for an exciting and innovative job abroad. Her dream job, she said. ('Above the professors' as she put it mischievously to me.)

It was only a week or so later that Melissa spun out, experiencing what might be called a psychotic episode, albeit in quite a mild form.

It took time with my supervisor to wonder whether there was perhaps a connection here.

What do we do when good things happen?

I am more alert to this now in working with clients (and indeed with myself). When a good thing happens, I don't assume that this will be uncomplicated for the person. How do they regard the good event? They may not feel that they deserve it even though it is what they have been longing and working for. It seems all sorts of unexpected feelings can be evoked by goodness coming your way. The response may not be what we might expect. Being given what we have longed for can be a delicate business that needs to be approached with care and support.

Perhaps close to this is the territory we have already dealt with regarding staying with goodness. When a person has had a troubled history, when little bits of goodness start emerging they may easily be skipped over and pushed to the margins, rather than being savoured, celebrated and rested in. Staying with goodness in these instances would be part of what I have spoken of as building up the healing vortex. For many of us, this is something that needs to be learnt and practised. One may gently remind the person of the good things that are happening or have happened, almost increasing their tolerance for this.

Similarly one might remind someone who really battles to be in the company of others: 'Remember recently you said you managed to speak freely at your music group and you had no bad after-effects. Things are improving.' The person can easily lose sight of this.[164] If there aren't enough 'bad' things to bring to therapy, the person may wonder if they're wasting their time. Not at all. Bringing good things can be at least as important – at times even more so – than sharing the difficulties. I try to remember to educate clients about this.

Many people begin consulting a psychotherapist in a time of crisis. There may have been a critical health event and you nearly died. Or you have become aware of your risk-taking behaviour – perhaps regarding sex, alcohol or drugs. After a few months, this immediate situation may change and you may be somewhat more settled. One could easily leave therapy at this point. However, the initial questions that arose in the time of crisis – questions such as 'how do I want to live my life?' – may remain unresolved. It can be worthwhile to continue the enquiry at this point. There can be a lovely spaciousness and openness in the work when one isn't dealing with an immediate crisis. Responsive support can be extremely valuable once the eye of the storm has passed. Why do we think we only need support in the hard times?

It may be that a sort of plateau is reached in the work and it is time for the client's system to experience a sense of rest for a while. This is important to honour. The person may think of ending therapy at this point, feeling that not much is happening. It may be good to gently encourage them to stay, explaining that after a period of quite intense work it can be good to experience therapy in a time when things are quieter, more at rest. It is beautiful if the person can allow this. In a way, one is celebrating the distance the person has come. I am not saying that breaks from therapy cannot be excellent and the time may come to end the therapy. But continuing with therapy when one is in a state of plateau or rest can be useful. One is getting to know a quieter place. It is a time to digest and integrate the changes that have taken place.

Reflection:

Do you have a suspicion that you might struggle to allow good things to happen and to embrace them? If so, you're definitely not alone in this.

What do you feel about the encouragement to have support in the 'good' times too?

When things are going along just fine – a sort of plateau period – how are you with this?

PART
5

Creativity and psychotherapy

I don't regard the territory of creativity and psycho-therapy as being far from each other. Approaching a fresh piece of paper on which to draw or write. Showing up for the next session with the client. Who is he today? Who am I? Each moment in the session a fresh one.

I wander out onto my front *stoep*.[165] There are the swallows, surely 60 this time, arranged along the telephone wires.

When I first noticed them about two weeks ago, I wondered why their image on the wire struck me so. Later I realised they looked like notes of music strung out along lined manuscript paper.[166]

By looking at where the birds are on the wires, I can sing the music I see. I can sing the birds.

Reflection:

What areas of creativity are you involved with at present? (This can include things such as baking, gardening...)

Are there creative pursuits you engaged in as a child, or at other times of your life, that you've let slip away? What would it be like to bring them back?

It's all an enquiry

Carl Jung spent the last half of his life using himself as a sort of laboratory, living experimentally and reflecting on his experience. His more significant work came from this period. Can we be this interested in ourselves – and so in humanity?

I spoke at the beginning of this book about Core Process – indeed life – being an enquiry. The Buddhist teacher and writer Martine Batchelor suggests:

> The most important part of the practice is for the question to remain alive and for your whole body and mind to become a question. In Zen they say that you have to ask with the pores of your skin and the marrow of your bones. A Zen saying points out: great questioning, great awakening; little questioning, little awakening; no questioning, no awakening.[167]

Don't look for sureness. It can be important *not* to have the answer. It might get in the way. Keep the enquiry open. Don't use force. Knowing arises. Let the energy of life do its work.

What the practitioner is offering in Core Process Psychotherapy is staying in the present moment with the client without judgement. This is a rare gift. There is no agenda – not even that of being helpful. The need to fix or change something can interrupt the sense of resting in the moment.

In this enquiry, you might want to notice the following:

- Can you give whatever arises equal attention?

- Can you pay equal attention to 'interesting' and 'not-interesting' bits?

- How your own likes and dislikes can pull your attention and in subtle ways direct a session.

- How you add something or take something away from the experience.

- Can you tolerate not understanding, not knowing?

- Can you resist interpreting?

- Can you allow a continual beginner's mind?[168]

In therapeutic work, simple questions like 'how do you know you're nervous?' can be useful. A person might say they're anxious or nervous or name another emotion. 'How do you know this?' sounds quite silly but can yield interesting responses. One sometimes discovers together that it wasn't nervousness at all. What feels like a nervous sensation in one's body could equally be a sense of anticipation or excitement. The attitude of enquiry, slowing things down, not taking things at face value, is so rewarding.

Pema Chodron in her inimitable way puts it like this:

> We could [stop] feeling that we must come up with a solution to a problem – or feeling that there is a solution or a problem at all.[169]

This can be a huge relief.

In a similar vein, Laura Donington speaks of her experience as a practitioner:

> If sadness comes up [in client work], I do not immediately seek for an object or cause, but I wait with that feeling.[170]

Techniques, she says, are used only in service of this process.[171]

A core process psychotherapy session can actually look outrageously ordinary. I remember volunteering during my training to do an individual session with Franklyn while the rest of our training group of about fourteen observed. That was what struck me about the session. It was just so ordinary. Here I was sitting with the great man and he did nothing spectacular. No special effects or techniques. Just me and him sitting together. Later – as now – I could sense the absolute beauty of this. There was nothing he was putting in the way between us. Just him and me. That takes trust from the therapist. There's a certain nakedness to it.

Reflection:

The open-ness of enquiry can have a waking up quality. Can you sense this?

Spiritual friendship

There is a conversation between the Buddha and Ananda, his faithful attendant and friend, that has not, I feel, been given adequate attention. It goes like this:

> Ananda was once thinking to himself that the practice of monastic life depended half on good friends and half on his own effort, so he said to the Buddha, 'This is half of the holy life, that is, good friendship, good companionship, and good comradeship.' The Buddha replied, 'Not so, Ananda. Not so, Ananda. This is the entire holy life, Ananda, that is, good friendship, good companionship, and good comradeship.'[172]

What are the implications if friendship is so central to life?

How will we build our capacity for loving relationship in this time of electronic connecting and the malaise in relationship with which I began this book? We each have a need for what you might call spiritual friendship – people with whom we can share the truth of who we are. Thomas Keating, in his classic *Open heart, Open mind*, says that 'spiritual friendship involving genuine self-disclosure is an essential ingredient for happiness.'[173]

As well as the possibility of increasing people's capacity to be in wise relationship, perhaps the therapeutic relationship itself can be seen as a form of spiritual friendship. Maura speaks movingly of this towards the end of her article *Licking Honey from the Razor's edge*:

> Psychotherapy needs to be truthful. It needs to really take on the conditions of the world... We need to reframe psychotherapy and we also have to reframe the notion of what and who a psychotherapist is... We need to start by trying to reframe the notion of psychotherapy more openly as *Dharma* friend. A *Dharma* friend is usually seen as someone who helps us in our search for reality and truthfulness. A *Dharma* friend offers companionship on the path of awakening, of coming into the moment. *Dharma* friendship

gives more of a flavour to this movement of the changing nature of psychotherapy. We need to try and shift
the notion of the psychotherapist as
being psychological, clinical and ob-
jective. The work is to bring us back
into human kindness... and... human
relationship.[174]

In building friendship, there are resources to
draw on such as the emphasis on community in
Christianity and the practice of *ubuntu* in African
society – *a person is a person through other people*. I have said that community development is
often seen as something for the poor and that it is
at least equally the richer of us who need to learn
the meaning of building real connection and to
slowly and experimentally learn to live together
better. No task could be more worthwhile.

I remember so well Maura saying that Thich Nhat
Hahn – the much-loved Vietnamese teacher –
spoke of the next Buddha as being the *sangha*.[175]
The *sangha* is a Sanskrit word referring to a gathering of friends – something like the congregation.
The next Buddha will be the *sangha*. Surely this
must be so.

Reflection:

Do you sense a stirring and a *yes* to this call to learn again how to forge friendship in our time? Can you let this longing touch you?

The stranger

When you see a stranger, welcome him in. This phrase comes easily to mind. I think it's from the Bible.

It may be odd to see oneself as this stranger. But perhaps useful.

In a talk entitled *The Gift of Christmas* Rowan Williams, former Archbishop of Canterbury, suggests that we are at odds with ourselves, we are strange to ourselves.[176] So while there's a familiarity there is also this strangeness.

The Persian poet Hafiz writes: 'You will love again the stranger who was yourself.'[177]

The practice of psychotherapy and other forms of embodied presence in relationship can contribute to this restoration.

May each of us love again the stranger who was ourself.

Endnotes

1   Programme Handbook 2002 - 2003 (Widecombe-in-the-Moor: Karuna Institute, 2002), 1.

2   Ibid.

3   Sadly, this is something the West seems to be effectively exporting to the rest of the world.

4   Or, as Stephen Batchelor put it in his classic *Buddhism Without Beliefs*, its origins can be understood (London: Bloomsbury,1997), 4.

5   Or, as Stephen says, can be let go of, ibid., 4.

6   Batchelor: There is a path that can be cultivated, ibid.,4.

7   In Pali, *anicca, dukkha* and *anatta* and *anitya, dukkha* and *anatman* in Sanskrit. These characteristics are profound and I'm abbreviating their meaning hugely for the purpose of this text. *Anatta* is often translated as no-self.

8   For more on this, read the first chapter of Stephen Batchelor's *Buddhism Without Beliefs* which was a set-work book in our first year.

9   In Ian Rees' very helpful paper, *Buddhist Teachings and Core Process Psychotherapy*, Widecombe-in-the-Moor: Karuna Institute, (undated), 29.

10   Talk given at the *Mindfulness & Beyond* conference of the Association for Core Process Psychotherapists in London, April 24-26 2009.

11   Talk at Sharpham, Devon, England, February 7, 2006.

12   Ibid.

13   Franklyn Sills speaking at the *Mindfulness & Beyond* conference.

14   Maura Sills is in conversation with Ros Oliver, *Psychotherapy as a spiritual journey*, View Issue 3 (1995): 44.

15   Ibid., 49.

16   Maura Sills, *Licking Honey from the Razor's Edge* in *The Psychology of Awakening,* ed. Gay Watson et al. (London: Rider, 1999), 188.

17   Ibid.

18   Ibid., 190.

19   In a Karuna flyer advertising a workshop by Maura Sills in 2013.

20   Maura Sills, *Psychotherapy as a Spiritual Journey,* 45.

21   Maura Sills speaks about this in her presentation at the *Mindfulness & Beyond* conference in 2009.

22   Rick Hanson and Richard Menduis, *Buddha's Brain: the practical neuroscience of happiness, love and wisdom* (Oakland: New Harbinger Publications, 2009), 93-5.

23   Maura makes herself available to work with people in acute distress. Sometimes this work can leave one with some of the feelings of the person you have been working with – hence Maura experiencing herself as perhaps worthless. But I am over-simplifying things here.

24   This is a programme called SAGE which was offered by the National Health Service in England.

25   Sadly, her relationship with her mom had broken down. Her mother had not believed her when she told her what was happening at home.

26   After writing this, I see that somewhere Franklyn writes very briefly about resourcing regulating the body.

27   Ian Rees speaks of the *brahmaviharas* being found in all schools of Buddhism but I've certainly met many Buddhists who haven't heard of them. *Buddhist Teachings and Core Process Psychotherapy,17.*

28   *Buddhist Teachings and Core Process Psychotherapy*, 17 and 19.

29   See Sue Gerhardt's moving book, *Why love matters: How Affection Shapes a baby's Brain* (London:

Routledge, 2003).

30   Talk on retreat entitled *The Coalescence of Compassion*, Gaia House, Devon, England, May 11-13, 2007.

31   Sonu Shamdasani, ed. C G Jung, *The Red Book: Liber novus* (New York: W W Norton, c 2009), 215.

32   I use this in the sense of supporting their inherent freedom, health and wellbeing.

33   Maura Sills, *Licking Honey from the Razor's Edge* in *The Psychology of Awakening,* ed. Gay Watson et al. (London: Rider,1999), 90.

34   Ibid.

35   From one of her talks – I think at the Karuna Institute. I don't have the exact source but she says this sort of thing frequently.

36   Maura Sills at the Gaia House retreat.

37   She felt these practices were not suited to the western disposition which she regarded as different from that of the East.

38   Maura Sills at Gaia House retreat.

39   Africa has a lot to teach us here.

40   Maura Sills touched on this too at the retreat I have mentioned.

41   There are practices where you are asked to send *metta* to yourself, to loved ones and to your enemies.

42   See Stephen Batchelor, *Buddhism Without Beliefs*, 5.

43   Chodron, *When Things Fall Apart. Heart Advice for Difficult Times*, 18.

44   In a talk at Sharpham, Totnes, Devon, England February 7, 2006.

45   In a talk on a retreat, Gaia House.

46   Ibid.

47   She went on to do one of the intensive trainings offered by the Karuna Institute, an MA in Mindfulness Based Psychotherapy. Information on the hermitage in South Africa that she founded with her husband Kittisaro can be found at http://www.dharmagiri.org.

48   Batchelor is controversial in some circles in that he critiques Buddhism being institutionalised as a religion. (Batchelor, *Buddhism Without Beliefs*,12).

49   Batchelor, *Buddhism Without Beliefs,* 6.

50   Maura Sills, *Psychotherapy as a spiritual journey*, 48.

51   Chodron, *When Things Fall* Apart,17.

52   Batchelor, *Buddhism Without Beliefs*, 7.

53   Ibid., xi.

54   Chodron, *When Things Fall Apart*, 78.

55   Laura Donington, *Core Process Psychotherapy* in *Innovative Therapy – A Handbook,* ed. David Jones (Maidenhead: Open University Press,1994), 65.

56   Maura Sills, in *Licking Honey from the Razor's Edge*, 187.

57   His essay on *Coretalk, the forum for Core Process Psychotherapists*, April 23, 2009.

58   *Buddhist Teachings and Core Process Psychotherapy*, 16.

59   Talk dated May 20, 2009. I was sent a transcription by a colleague but am unsure where the talk was delivered.

60   Donington, *Core Process Psychotherapy*, 53.

61   Maura Sills, in *Licking Honey from the Razor's Edge*,190.

62   Ibid., 190.

63   Ibid., 191.

64   *World Christian Community for Meditation*, March 11, 2015.

65   The *Sutta* (Pali) or *Sutra* (Sanskrit) is a collection of the Buddha's teaching. These were first memorised and then written down several hundred years after his death. This information is from Kittisaro and Thanissara, *Listening to the Heart*, 2014, Berkeley North Atlantic Books p 254.

66   June 29, 2014.

67   On the Karuna website: http://www.karuna-institute.co.uk.

68   This is a reference from Franklyn Sills that I picked up on the Karuna Institute website.

69   Transcription of a talk by Franklyn Sills dated May 20, 2009.

70   Presence and Perception notes (Widecombe-in-the-Moor: Karuna Institute, undated), 3.

71   Presence and Perception, 1.

72   Literally the definition of a fulcrum is the still point on which a lever rests. I imagine this as the midpoint of a see-saw. I am drawing this exercise from Franklyn Sill's work.

73   Some of these are terms that Franklyn uses.

74   I do often find the medical model intimidating. Which isn't to say there aren't stunning health workers within this sector.

75   Franklyn speaks of this in his presentation at the *Mindfulness & Beyond* conference in 2009.

76   Rees, *Buddhist Teachings and Core Process Psychotherapy*, 16.

77   In her teaching at the Karuna Institute.

78   October 27, 2014.

79   Franklyn Sills, *Presence and Perception, 1.* (a paper/ handout).

80   Ibid., 1.

81   This is an analogy used by Maura Sills in her talk at the *Mindfulness & Beyond* conference.

82   *Mindfulness & Beyond* conference.

83   A retreat offered in Hout Bay, Cape Town, by Martine and Stephen Batchelor, January 25-27, 2002.

84   These visits were between 1920 and 1925. Jung was making an observation then that I feel remains valid.

85   Meredith Sabini, ed., *The Earth has a Soul: Nature Writings of CG Jung.* (Berkeley: North Atlantic Books, 2002), 108.

86   Soma is another word for body.

87   Rees, *Buddhist Teachings and Core Process Psychotherapy*, 17.

88   Ibid., 17, referring to a statement by Maura Sills.

89   At a SAAJA seminar given in Cape Town, South Africa, on October 13, 2012, entitled *The embodied Psyche*.

90   Maura Sills, *Psychotherapy as a spiritual journey,* 48-49.

91   Ibid., 48.

92   *The Body Remembers: The Psychophysiology of Trauma and Trauma Treatment* is the title of a very useful book by Babette Rothschild (New York: W.W. Norton & Company, 2000).

93   Talk at Sharpham, February 7, 2006.

94   The international Buddhist teacher I have referred to before.

95   My translation.

96   In this section, I have referred a few times to a hand-out *Exchanges: an introduction* by Maxine Linnell from the foundation phase of the training.

97   Donington, *Core Process Psychotherapy*, 50.

98   I include here people like myself who are the wealthy living in poorer countries.

99   I am alluding to a statement made by the interesting author Charles Eisenstein speaking of the mental anguish experienced in the West – and, he says, we're 'the winners'.

100   This is a handout entitled *Presentation on Path Out of Poverty Programme, Goedgedacht Trust – A Rural Development Model* from a presentation given by Elsabe O'Leary in August 2014 in Cape Town. She includes an extract from a book entitled *People first. A guide to self-reliant, participatory rural development,* Stan Burkey, 1993, and the part that I have included comes from this.

101   (Cape Town: Hands-On Books, 2013), 34.

102   This is the title of a book of his published in 1986.

103   Groves, *Pleasure-in-relating*, 66.

104   Mail & Guardian October 24-30, 2014, 39.

105   http://www.youtube.com/watch?v=HDVhZHJagfQ&

app=desktop.

106   Donington, *Core Process Psychotherapy*, 55.

107   Franklyn Sills, *Draft Sections on neural issues, trans-marginal stress and attachment* (Widecombe-in-the-Moor: Karuna Institute, undated), 11.

108   Franklyn Sills ibid., 13. Sills is also making reference to Frank Lake's work here.

109   Sharpham talk, February 7, 2006.

110   Franklyn Sills, *Draft sections on neural issues, trans-marginal stress and attachment*, 9.

111   Cape Town 2001-2.

112   Jonny Steinberg, *A Man of Good Hope* (Cape Town: Jonathan Ball, 2015), 5-6.

113   Ibid., 5.

114   Ibid, 98.

115   Ibid, 321.

116   *Zen Dust* (Johannesburg: Jacana Media, 2012), 39-40.

117   *Cherishing the Wound* – unpublished at the time of writing.

118   *Muhammad: A Prophet for our Time* (London: Harper Perennial, 2006), 36.

119   I am aware that this is a generalisation and that these distinctions are fluid and changing.

120   In *Mail & Guardian*, Friday section May 10-16 2013.

121   Steinberg, *A Man of Good Hope*, 191.

122   'The suit didn't fit perfectly then and neither does it today,' were his words. (Cape Town: Jonathan Ball, 2014), 106.

123   I am drawing here on my notes from a talk given by Maura Sills at Sharpham on February 7, 2006.

124   This was part of a thanksgiving ritual.

125   Talk at Sharpham, May 7, 2006.

126   *Mindfulness & Beyond* conference, 2009.

127   Food security is the concern as to whether there will be enough food for everyone due to climatic changes.

128   Transition Town Totnes mailing, May 20, 2014.

129 Uploaded in June 2007.

130 *When Things Fall Apart*, 121.

131 Lucia Capaldi, www.totnestherapy.co.uk/Fun-andGames

132 Peter Levine's earlier work is *Waking the Tiger* and his more recent and personal book is titled *In an Unspoken Voice*. Babette Rothschild has written *The Body Remembers*. These are all useful for the reader who wants to learn more about this territory.

133 Handout, *'Notes for working with edges of overwhelm'*, Year 1 2002, Anne Oversee and Angela Willow.

134 Franklyn Sills, *'The COEX System'*, handout (Widecombe-in-the-Moor: Karuna Institute, undated), 1. He is referring to Stanislav Grof's work.

135 Maura Sills clinical support day, October 1, 2007. A talk entitled *How to recognise shock in yourself and your clients and how to respond*.

136 Maura Sills, *Licking Honey from the Razor's Edge*, 193.

137 In the early section on resourcing.

138 I am drawing here on notes from a colleague Anna Colgan from the Somatic Experiencing training, another excellent training in working with trauma, that is based on the work of Peter Levine.

139 *Core Process Psychotherapy*, 65.

140 *The Body Remembers*, 92-3.

141 Ibid., 88.

142 An article from *Guardian Professional*, October 2, 2014, by Jo Confino received in a mailing of the Inner Transition group of Transition Town Totnes, October 7, 2014. The author is referring to the work of Patrician McCabe of New Mexico and Arizona.

143 Frank questions are to be welcomed in therapy – as are accusations and whatever else arises in 'talking back' to the therapist. This is not always comfortable of course.

144 Posted on coretalk, the online forum for core process

psychotherapists, in 2001.

145   *The Core Process Trauma Booklet* (Widecombe-in-the-Moor: Karuna Institute, undated), 26.

146   *The Core Process Trauma Booklet,* 26.

147   *Core Process Psychotherapy*, 55.

148   These strategies were developed by William Reich.

149   For further information, you could look at Ron Kurtz, *Body-Centred Psychotherapy, the Hakomi Method* (Mendocino: LifeRhythm,1990).

150   In a flyer for a Kum Nye retreat she offered at the Karuna Institute in October 2014. Kum Nye is a movement form.

151   Maura Sills, *Psychotherapy as a spiritual journey*, 44.

152   I think this sentence is from Maura or Franklyn Sills but I cannot find the source.

153   Franklyn Sills, training notes (Widecombe-in-the-Moor: Karuna Institute, undated).

154   Transcription of a talk dated May 20, 2009.

155   Franklyn Sills handout, *Core Process and Personality Shaping* (Widecombe-in-the-Moor: Karuna Institute, undated), 5 and 6.

156   I am unable to source this quote. It is from one of the references I have already used.

157   *Core Process Psychotherapy*, 65.

158   *Psychotherapy as a spiritual journey*, 46.

159   *About a Body: Working with the Embodied mind in psychotherapy*, UKCP conference, September ,10-12, 2004, 4.

160   '*Psychotherapy* as a spiritual journey,' 46.

161   Ibid., 46.

162   *Licking Honey from the Razor's Edge*, 193.

163   Ibid., 194.

164   This isn't to imply one doesn't enquire further into this territory but it's good to celebrate the small successes. This client and I do sometimes touch into the longing that lies behind her anxiety around social contact with others. From living an extremely

isolated life, her being longs for contact.

165   Veranda.

166   The paper one uses for writing music.

167   *'What is This?' Tricycle: The Buddhist Review,* October 27, 2012.

168   For these useful pointers, I am drawing on a hand-out, *Sustained Attention*, from the foundation phase of the training, undated.

169   *When Things Fall Apart*, 130.

170   *Core Process Psychotherapy*, 59.

171   Ibid., 63.

172   http://www.londonbuddhistvihara.org/samadhi/May2003.htm.

173   Twentieth Anniversary Edition 2006, 162.

174   195-6. The word *Dharma* translates as the teachings or the nature of reality.

175   Gaia House retreat, May 11-13, 2007.

176   London, December 19, 2014.

177   Hafiz is a 14th century Persian poet who has been brought to the world by the suitably playful presence and translation of Daniel Ladinsky. I found this quote in an article by Kim Rosen, *'The Healing Power of Poetry,' Spirituality and Health,* September/October, 2012.

Books by the same author:

Pleasure-in-relating
Cherishing the Wound

Printed in Great Britain
by Amazon